VANCOUVER ISLAND

THE ISLAND SERIES

*Corsica
†Harris and Lewis
  The Isle of Arran
†The Isle of Mull
  Lundy
  The Maltese Islands
†Orkney
  St Kilda and other Hebridean Outliers
*Vancouver

in preparation
*The Falklands
*Fiji
*Grand Bahama
*Sardinia
*The Seychelles
†Shetland
*Singapore
†Skye

* Published in the United States by Stackpole

† Published in the United States by David & Charles

VANCOUVER ISLAND

by S. W. JACKMAN

DAVID & CHARLES : NEWTON ABBOT

STACKPOLE BOOKS : HARRISBURG

This edition first published in 1972
in Great Britain by David & Charles (Publishers) Limited,
Newton Abbot, Devon
in the United States by Stackpole Books, Harrisburg, Pa.

ISBN 0 7153 5499 x (*Great Britain*)
ISBN 0 8117 1848 4 (*United States*)
Library of Congress No 74–179611

© S. W. JACKMAN 1972

*Set in eleven on thirteen point Baskerville
and printed in Great Britain by
Clarke Doble & Brendon Limited Plymouth*

Magistro Sociisque
Collegii Pembrochiani Cantabrigiensis
Grato Animo

CONTENTS

Cape
Scott

Port Hardy

Malcolm I.

Alert
Bay

Port
McNeill

Quatsino
Sound

Port
Alice

*Nimpkish
L.*

Kelsey
Bay

Cape
Cook

*Kyuquot
Sound*

Campbell

*Nootka
I.*

Gold
River

7219 △
Golden Hinde

*Nootka
Sound*

P a c i f i c   O c e a n

*Clayoquot
Sound*

Tofino

Ucluelet

VANCOUVER
ISLAND

0   10   20 miles 30   40   50

0   10   20 km 30   40   50

+ + + Railway   - - - - - Road

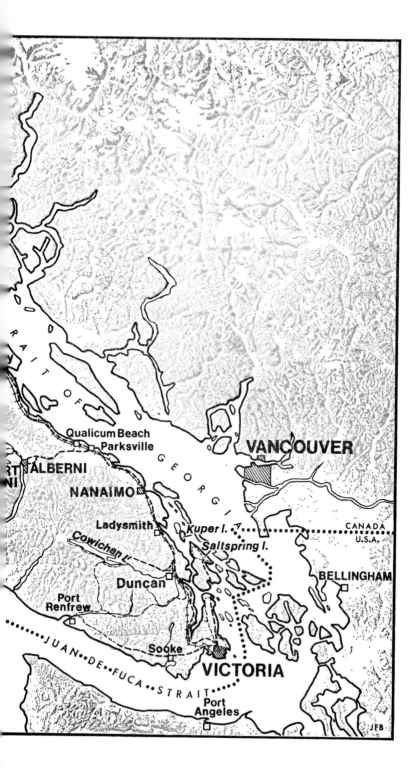

ILLUSTRATIONS

ILLUSTRATIONS

IN TEXT

With one exception shown above all the photographic illustrations are by courtesy of the Government of British Columbia.

The map of Vancouver Island is by John Bryant.

The map showing the major reserves is by courtesy of the Government of British Columbia.

The drawing of the Indian plank house is by Pedro Guedes, to whom the author and publishers are indebted.

1 INTRODUCTION—the island and its physical developments

OF the many islands lying off the coast of western North America, by far the largest is Vancouver Island. Its latitude is 48° 18′33″N to 50° 52′36″N; its longitude 123° 15′49″W to 128° 25′51″W. If one flew directly from one end of the island to another the distance would be approximately 280 miles. Making a similar flight across the island at its widest point one would travel about 85 miles. In shape, then, Vancouver Island is rather like a somewhat stubby cigar.

It may well come as a surprise to many people to discover that Vancouver Island is so large. Indeed, its land mass is some 12,400 square miles—this is exclusive of the numerous islands which lie well within the many inlets and bays of the main island. If these extra portions of land are added, and they probably should be, then the total area is 13,250 square miles. Yet all of this only makes up something like 3·7 per cent of the total area of the vast province of British Columbia. The population in 1971 is approximately 375,000 or about 11 per cent of British Columbia.

As yet it is impossible to drive the entire length of the island on a public road. On the eastern coast there is a paved road from Victoria to Kelsey Bay—a distance of 250 miles. Indeed, it may be many years before it will be possible to drive all around the island. By the time such a road system is developed other forms of transport than the automobile will have been produced, and the need for such a road become non-existent. At any time the cost of road construction along the entire west coast would be extremely high and probably prohibitive.

13

INTRODUCTION

The eastern and western coasts of Vancouver Island are vastly different. The western side has many inlets similar to fjords in Norway. These inlets are often very deep, eg Alberni Inlet 1,125ft, Muchlat Inlet 1,150ft and Kyuquot Sound 860ft. As would be expected, the western coastline is extremely rugged, with cliffs and rocky outcroppings. On the other hand, the eastern side has fewer inlets and the land mass slopes towards the sea more gently. Consequently, the best beaches for bathing are to be found on the eastern side of the island. Also, the water in the Strait of Georgia is warmer than the open Pacific.

Through the central *massif* of the island there is a range of mountains with peaks of considerable height : Golden Hinde is 7,219ft, Elkhorn is 7,190ft and Victoria 7,075ft. In fact, most of the island is more than 500ft above sea level, though the chief population centres are generally close to sea level.

In earlier times the island was part of the sea bottom, but a series of volcanic eruptions pushed the land upward out of the water. Probably at this period the island was all part of the mainland of North America, but gradually the two areas were to become distinct entities. During the Ice Age, when great glaciers —often over 6,000ft thick—covered the island, the general structure of the island took shape. Valleys, inlets, lakes, mountains were all either affected or created by the moving ice. With the departure of the glaciers the land rose up again, but the glaciers left great deposits of boulders and gravel everywhere. Consequently, the general soil structure is directly related to the age of the glacier, and the soil in Vancouver Island is very varied. It is estimated that there are approximately 420,000 acres of land capable of being successfully farmed. The rest of the soil is of sub-marginal value for agriculture.

A quick glance at the map will show that Vancouver Island is dotted with lakes of varying size. Moreover, the lakes are not confined to particular areas. In the north, for example, are the Nimpkish, Bonanza and Woss Lakes; in the central part of the island, Comox, Campbell, Kennedy, Great Central and Sproat Lakes; and in the southern section, the Cowichan, Shawnigan and Sooke Lakes. There are many other smaller lakes as well. Inevitably, the central mountain range determines the direction of the drainage basins. There is no one great river on the island but, like the lakes, many rivers of varying size. The Nimpkish, Campbell, Somass, Salmon, Gold, Nanaimo, Nitinat and Cowichan are reckoned to be the chief rivers. Between them they drain about one third of the total area. All the rivers and lakes offer excellent fishing. On Vancouver Island is also one of the highest waterfalls in the world, with a drop of 1,443ft. Unfortunately, the Della Falls are not very accessible : one must go 24 miles by boat up Great Central Lake and then 12 miles more over a fairly rugged trail, but once reached, all the effort is forgotten in the spectacular beauty of the waterfall.

CLIMATE

Vancouver Island has three distinct climatological zones. The north and west coasts are wet, the south and east coasts are dry—both zones are temperate—and the central mountains are both wet and cool. It must be stated emphatically that Vancouver Island's climate is quite unlike that which people generally assume to be typically Canadian, since the island is not covered with snow for months on end. The extremely moderate climate is largely influenced by the Pacific Ocean. In particular, this means that the west coast is usually warmer in winter. However, nowhere in the island are what could be called sharp shifts of season and temperature. The average rainfall in Victoria is 27·35in, the wetter months being December and January. On the other hand, at Zeballos on the west coast the average rainfall is 255·11in. At Qualicum on the east coast, about midway between Victoria and Port Hardy, the precipitation is 70·77in. At Port Hardy itself the rainfall is 92·82in. The amount of average snowfall is similar : Victoria 5·3in, Zeballos 50·4in, Qualicum 11·2in and Port Hardy 39·8in. On the other hand, snowfall on the moun-

15

INTRODUCTION

tains can be quite considerable. At Forbidden Plateau, the chief skiing area on the island, snow depth has been measured up to 18ft.

The annual mean temperatures for various segments of the island are remarkably similar: Victoria 50°F (10°C), Zeballos 49°F (9·5°C), Qualicum 48°F (9°C) and Port Hardy 46°F (8°C). The maxima and minima are likewise not dissimilar: Victoria 96°F (36°C) and 7°F (−14°C), Zeballos 80°F (27°C) and 11°F (−12°C), Qualicum 82°F (28°C) and 11°F (−12°C) and Port Hardy 83°F (28° C) and 60°F (16°C). Yet, it must be pointed out that Cumberland, well above the forty-ninth parallel, has extremes of 111°F (44°C) to −5°F (−21°C), while Campbell River, which is on the fiftieth parallel of latitude, varies from a high of 96°F (36° C) to a low of 7°F (−14°C). To summarise all of this information simply is not difficult. The coastal areas, regardless of latitude, are similar in temperature, while inland communities—and they may only be a few miles from the sea—have greater differences between highs and lows.

Even more interesting are the variations in hours of sunlight in a year. The average for Victoria is 2,207, Campbell River 1,747, Alberni 1,481, Estevan Point 1,649. It will be clear from these figures that although Victoria may have a similar maximum temperature to, say, Campbell River, the number of hours of sunshine are somewhat different. Campbell River has 11 per cent less sunshine than Victoria. Alberni has a similar maximum temperature to Victoria—93°F (34°C) for the former, 96°F (36°C) for the latter—but the hours of sunshine are not comparable. Alberni has only 67 per cent as many hours of sunshine in a year as Victoria.

Nevertheless, Vancouver Island has remarkably equitable weather. Wind is a problem, and there are generally half a dozen good gales each year, with wind blowing above 40mph. Victoria and Port Hardy rarely have more than thirty-five foggy days in a year.

The consequences of such a mild climate are obvious. The growing season begins in late February, but, since there is no

16

Page 17 (above) Tree covered lake shores and high hills are major features of island ecology. Both coniferous and deciduous trees as well as low bush grow abundantly; *(below)* the petroglyphs are all that remain of a mysterious civilisation and a people lost to the annals of history. Petroglyphs can be seen south of Nanaimo, on the cliffs at Nitinat Lake, at Tofino and Sooke as well as a few other places on the island

Page 18 (above) 'The Butter Church'—so-called because the builders were paid for the labour in butter—is now only a shell but it stands as a stark memorial to the work of early missionaries; (below) Craigflower Manor, built in the early 1850s by Kenneth Mackenzie, reflects the traditions of the pioneer in Eastern Canada and also earlier Scottish antecedents

period of great heat, general development is slow. Vancouver Island is almost unique in all of Canada. It alone has a climate which makes it especially attractive as a place for retirement. As a result the island has always had many people who settle after active careers elsewhere. Prior to the 1939–45 war, immigrants came from all over what was then the Empire and from Great Britain as well. Latterly this has not been the case; instead, Vancouver Island has become the 'Florida of Canada' and elderly people, from the prairies in particular, now come to take advantage of the mild winter weather.

One of the first things which strikes any stranger to the island is the luxuriant growth. Indeed, an aerial view shows it to be densely covered with forest. The open spaces are few and far between, particularly in the central and northern sections of the island.

The Douglas fir grows almost everywhere but is at its best in areas that are less subjected to excessive rainfall. The Douglas fir often attains 300ft in height and is truly majestic. The Sitka spruce is also common. This species often attains 200ft in height with a diameter of 10ft. The hemlock which flourishes in the rain forest terrain of the west coast may sometimes be as tall as 150ft with a diameter of 3–4ft. Other conifers found on Vancouver Island are red and yellow cedars, balsam fir and pine.

After an area has been logged over initially it looks a picture of devastation, but then the red alder, a deciduous tree of fast growth, often grows prolifically in such terrain. The red maple flourishes in similar circumstances. The alder and the maple are attractive trees and in other areas are often planted as windbreaks to serve until the slower-growing conifers develop.

The Garry oak thrives on well drained sites. This oak is seen more frequently in the environs of Victoria and in the Cowichan Valley. It also grows well in the neighbouring Gulf Islands. It

B

19

is a tree with no commercial use, but it is highly ornamental.
Legend has it that the Garry oak, which is also found in Oregon
and Washington, was brought by early Spanish explorers.

The only broad leaf evergreen native to Canada, the arbutus,
grows in many of the same areas as the Garry oak. Like the
latter, the arbutus has no economic value; it too, is purely decorative. It sheds its leaves in the summer, and many a gardener
complains about the chore of sweeping these up—the more so
since they rot very slowly and consequently are of little use in
the making of compost. The arbutus also sheds its bark.
The tree is at its best in mid-winter and early spring. Then the
dark green leaves glistening in the pale sunshine and the bark
with its smooth reddish colour combine to make it extremely
handsome.

The Pacific dogwood is the native flower of British Columbia
and its official emblem. Though prevalent on the northern part
of the island, it does not grow in great numbers and is found more
often in isolation. The flower, though very charming, is not in fact
a flower in the proper botanical sense of the word. Many people
plant dogwood trees in their gardens, but those just uprooted from
the forest rarely do well. The best ornamental dogwood come
from nurseries, and even these have to be carefully nurtured.

On the west coast in particular, but wherever there is moisture
enough, salal is ubiquitous. This shrub-like plant with dark green
leaves provides a wonderful ground cover. Normally it does not
grow more than a foot or two, but on the west coast in the rain-
forest climate it grows very quickly and attains considerable
height—5ft is not unusual—and becomes so thick that it is virtually impassable. The salal is cut in vast quantities and shipped
to florists in eastern Canada to make wreaths and other floral
pieces.

All over the island broom (genista) blossoms add a touch of
colour in late spring. The broom is not native. It was, so the story
goes, brought to Victoria by Sir Joseph Trutch, the first
lieutenant-governor. Whatever its origin, it has taken to Vancouver Island with enthusiasm. Gorse is found in and around

Victoria but, like broom, it is not native and it does not seem to have spread as much.

There are always wild flowers somewhere. The dogtooth violet, the erythronium, the brilliant blue camas—the Indians ate the bulb—the trillium and the delightful calypso or ladys slipper as well as many others appear each spring. Throughout the rest of the year the woodsides and meadows are enhanced with equally colourful blossoms. The ubiquitous Californian poppy is seen along the roadside all over the island. Its golden yellow orange colour cannot fail to please even the most jaundiced eye.

Many non-native shrubs and plants have been brought to the island over the years. Some of these, like the broom, have gone 'native'. Others appear only in the many handsome gardens. There are very few wild rhododendrons, for example. However, the beautiful wild red rhododendron, a great rarity in British Columbia, is found near Parksville. Near Ucluelet there are many rhododendrons, but all of these were originally cultivated varieties which have seeded and spread.

FAUNA

Because Vancouver Island is still relatively unpopulated and in 'a state of nature', indigenous animal life continues. The local black bear wanders about freely almost everywhere. Of course, it is not seen often within the urban centres, but any hiker or camper is bound to meet a bear sooner or later. They are not generally dangerous except when they have cubs or shortly after a long winter's hibernation. Nevertheless, the black bear can be very annoying to campers for it is extremely curious. It forages about on camp sites looking for food, and the unwary camper who has failed to secure his gear and supplies may return to find them in a dreadful mess.

There are still cougars (mountain lion or puma) in the more remote parts. The cougar is reputedly quite ferocious, but as it rarely comes near centres of population it is unlikely to be harmful. To be sure, a cougar was shot on the steps of the library in

Victoria not long ago, but this was a fluke. The cougar prefers the dark wooded areas to bright city lights. Periodically, a cougar may attack cattle or sheep, but this, too, is infrequent. The cougar prefers deer as a prey.

Curiously enough, Vancouver Island has some animals, or rather particular species, which are not found elsewhere. The Columbian or black-tail deer roams the island. This deer is smaller than those on the mainland and lacks the white-rump patch. Deer—stags only—are shot in the autumn and winter under a strict system of regulation. A licence must be obtained from the government, and a limit is placed on the number of stags that may be shot by any one individual. Indeed, all shooting—called hunting in Canada—is under governmental control.

Another purely indigenous animal is the local species of murem montis. This little creature is quite harmless. He differs only very slightly from his mainland brother, and to the layman's eye these variations are unnoticeable. It is perhaps a nice conceit, however, to know that the island has some animals which are not quite the same as elsewhere in Canada.

There are no mountain sheep, mountain goats, moose or caribou in the wild state. There are, however, a few Roosevelt elk. These, like the cougar, live in the remote northern and interior areas, being rarely seen by the populace at large. As with the black-tail deer, the elk are somewhat smaller than their main-land counterparts. The elk became almost extinct by 1968, and since then very severe restrictions were placed on shooting them. It is to be hoped that as a result the herd will be enlarged considerably in a few years.

Perhaps most surprising to the modern world is the fact that wolves can occasionally be seen on the island, though the number is exceedingly small. One was shot in 1968 north of Sayward. There is probably more talk about the existence of these wolves than fact. Periodically the newspapers report that packs of wolves have been seen, but upon investigation it is more frequently found that the so-called wolves are only dogs. The wolf is not a danger to society and is unlikely ever to be so.

All of the little animals—otter, muskrat, mink and beaver—that are found in British Columbia live on the island. The few rabbits are almost certainly descendants of domesticated ones that somehow managed to escape, or which at some time were deliberately let loose. There are some squirrels, but far more prevalent are the grey chipmunks. These small rodents are very impudent little animals, but they are very engaging at the same time.

To any ornithologist the island bird-life presents an infinite variety. A perusal of James Munro and Ian McTaggart Cowan on *Bird Fauna of British Columbia* will be well worth while. Eagles, owls, robins, cormorants, ducks, pigeons—all of the species found generally in western North America are seen on the island. Game birds flourish extremely well. Ruffed or willow grouse appear frequently in logged areas; the blue grouse favours logged off clearings. The ring-neck pheasant and the California quail have both been introduced with great success. The California quail, an engaging bird, is much in evidence in the environs of Victoria. Indeed, this bird does not seem to worry about humans and in most residential sections of Victoria makes itself quite at home. A quail and her chicks are a charming sight in many gardens. Game birds may be shot only during a specific season and upon the acquisition of a licence from the government. There is also a strict limitation on the number of birds which an individual may shoot in a day. Because there are so many lakes, inlets and tidal estuaries, sea birds are everywhere. Several varieties of gull, teal, widgeon, mallard, cormorant are readily observed. A walk along any of the beaches provides the ornithologist—young or old, amateur or professional—with much pleasure. The island is on the migratory route of both Canada geese and brant and these settle in great flocks during spring and autumn. Occasionally a snow goose is seen as well.

Each summer the humming bird adds a picturesque charm to

many gardens. This little bird is not evident in any large number but there are enough to ensure that few gardeners, particularly in the southern part of the island, can fail to see several. The wild canary adds a further note of colour to the horticultural scene.

The jolly woodpecker with his bright head and impudent manner can be seen almost everywhere. The ubiquitous crow makes his raucous sound from one end of the island to the other, and the robin is equally universal. The majestic and graceful bald eagle is found in considerable numbers, on both coasts and in the hinterland. The eagle has a good supply of food, and is in no danger of becoming extinct. It is protected by law from hunters.

A few non-game birds have been naturalised with varying degrees of success. The English sparrow is as cheeky in the New World as in his original habitat. The number of Japanese starlings once reached such proportions that they became a true agricultural pest. Shoots were organised for their limitation. In recent years the Japanese starling seems to have declined and the absolute number appears to be less. This is only partly the result of organised action by farmers; there is some thought that insecticides such as DDT have taken their toll as well. One bird which has been naturalised with limited success is the English skylark. It is to be found chiefly in Saanich. One of the favourite nesting places is a field in the grounds of the University of Victoria. Despite the fact that some five thousand-odd people pass within a few feet of this field every day, the skylark remains. Conservationists and students at the university alike are adamant that nothing shall disturb this bird. Petitions have been presented to the university authorities requesting that no buildings be constructed on the field where the skylark nests. So far the supporters of the skylark have been successful and as long as the present chancellor, Dr Roderick Haig-Brown—a well-known local conservationist—is in office, there is little likelihood that the bird will be disturbed. Since the citizens of Victoria like to claim that their city is a 'little bit of olde England', it adds a nice touch to have the only English skylarks in Canada.

24

FISH

Anyone wishing to know about the many sorts of fish to be found in the inshore waters of the island as well as in the lakes and rivers is well advised to consult Clifford G. Carl's various pamphlets and books published by the government of British Columbia. There are several species of salmon—the sockeye, the chinook or spring, the coho and the blue-back—which abound in large numbers. The rainbow trout occurs in most of the lakes and rivers; his sea-going brother, called a steelhead, is also relatively widespread. The local char—eastern brook trout—have been introduced with much success. They were first brought to the island about the turn of this century; indeed, it was approximately at the same time that the first rainbow trout were placed in British waters. Another form of trout—the cut-throat—inhabits both the rivers and the sea. There is also a small-mouth bass and the black bass, as well as kokanee in the larger lakes. In the sea itself there are ling cod and rock cod, halibut, skate and herrings among many others. The usual shellfish—oysters, clams, mussels —are quite plentiful, but only oysters and clams are used much for food. Attempts to introduce the lobster have thus far not proved very successful; of the local crustacea, the large Alaska crab provides the best alternative.

Each year in early September the oulachans or candlefish make their appearance. The oulachans are very small and somewhat oily, but excellent eating. The Indians used them also as a source of light. The pilchard, once very plentiful, seems to have vanished almost completely. Apparently the Indians predicted this would happen because of the fishing practices pursued by the white man.

There are seals on both the east and west coasts. They are the enemies of the fishermen since they destroy the salmon nets. They are often shot on sight by the white fishermen. The local seal is of no real commercial value, being generally the hair seal. Dogfish are almost as unpopular as seals. Single fish are generally killed and thrown back to feed the gulls. However, if they are caught on a large scale they may be used for fishmeal. The *Cethorinus*

25

maximus, a sort of shark, occasionally reaching 40ft in length, is sometimes seen, particularly in Saanich Inlet.

Schools of whales often appear in quite large numbers in the local waters at some time every year. The so-called 'killer whales' are also very prevalent. These are not really true whales in the proper generic sense.

Recently a number of 'killer whales' have been captured alive and placed in aquaria. A white 'killer whale', a great rarity, lives in captivity in Oak Bay. 'Killer whales' can be taught tricks and become very accomplished performers.

The island even has its own version of the Loch Ness Monster. It is called Cadborosaurus—from Cadboro Bay where it was first sighted and saurus because of its reptilian characteristics. When not in Cadboro Bay, Cadborosaurus presumably disports himself in the waters of the Strait of Juan de Fuca. He—the general assumption is that the beast is masculine in sex—was first sighted in the early 1930s. Periodically since that time there have been reports of his re-appearance. The belief in his existence is strongly held in many quarters, and like the Loch Ness Monster he is assumed to be real until proved otherwise.

LAND WEALTH

The mineral deposits on the island are extensive. Copper, molybdenum, silver, lead and iron exist in considerable quantities. There is still a certain amount of prospecting and exploratory work being done and this is particularly in evidence on the northern part of the island.

There are old Indian legends of gold in the Chemainus area, but nothing of significance has been discovered there. There was a brief flurry in 1863 when gold was discovered in a small river near Victoria. The early placer mining on what is now called Goldstream lasted only briefly. Soon after, further attempts were made to obtain gold from the quartz veins in the same general area. The amount of gold per ton of ore was negligible and the bubble soon burst. A bigger gold rush occurred in the summer of 1864. As a result of the exploration of Dr Robert Brown, gold was found in the Leech River, a tributary of the Sooke River. Wild reports reached Victoria, and, by August, a Leechtown came into existence. The community did not long survive. There was gold certainly, but not in great quantities. Occasionally there are still the odd newspaper accounts of gold in the Sooke River, but it is quite certain that no commercial goldmining is likely to ensue at any time.

Coal was first noted at Beaver Harbour in 1835, but actual production did not really begin until 1849. In order to protect the mine, Fort Rupert was built the same year. However, better coal was found at Nanaimo and the mine at Fort Rupert was abandoned. Fort Rupert itself gradually fell into total disuse, and has now disappeared almost completely. The mines at Nanaimo were first worked by the Hudson's Bay Company, but in due course various British controlled companies were promoted to take advantage of the discoveries. However, with the advent of Robert Dunsmuir, a local resident, and the rise of his empire the whole operation was vastly enlarged. Coal production increased from something like 20,000 tons per annum in the 1860s with a few hundred mines, to 550,000 tons by the mid-1890s with about 2,300 men working in the collieries.

Coal brought not only prosperity but also tragedy, eg, on 4 May 1887 there was a disaster at Nanaimo. 'The first intimation of an explosion . . . was a terrific shock followed by an outburst of thick black smoke from the air shaft. This was quickly followed by a recoil movement which was even more terrific than the first. In a few minutes flames commenced to issue from the air shaft, and with a loud roaring noise, arose many feet in the air.' Thus the *Colonist* reported the event which led to the death of between one and two hundred men and boys.

Coal created towns, some of which still survive, such as Ladysmith, Union Bay, Wellington and Cumberland. The hey-day of the collieries was just prior to the 1914–18 war. Gradually, other forms of fuel began to replace coal—particularly for private domestic use. The last operational coal mine on Vancouver

27

Island was at Tsable River. Its coal was shipped out of Buckley Bay. The Tsable River mine closed down in 1968; however, there is still a pile of coal at Buckley Bay as a mute reminder of the port.

An even more poignant survivor of the days when coal and prosperity were intimately connected is the ruined town of Cassidy. Founded early in this present century, at one time it had a theatre, shops, many houses and even a block of flats. In its hey-day it had 700 people. When mines closed in 1931, the populace began to drift away, and eventually the town was abandoned. The houses, gardens, streets are gradually disappearing; the buildings remain empty; Cassidy is a ghost town.

Cheap electrical power was one of the reasons for the decline of the coal industry. In the past decade expansion has taken place on a large scale. The British Columbia Hydro—the government owned and operated electrical power corporation—has generators which produce 339,600kW, of which 78 per cent is from hydro-electric plants. The largest of these plants, the John Hart Generating Station near Campbell River, alone produces 120,000kW. There are also some private generating plants— four hydro-electric, five steam, and one gas-diesel. The private companies generate 95,090kW. The steam generators, which are all privately owned, are in pulp mills where waste and recovered wood products offer a cheap fuel for steam generators.

PHYSICAL ENVIRONMENT

Something at this juncture should be said about the various islands—chiefly off the eastern coast—which may be considered dependent on Vancouver Island itself. These islands are similar to the main island in almost every fashion, being but smaller in size.

Saltspring, Mayne, Pender, Galiano and Saturna Islands would seem to be satellites of Victoria. Slightly to the north are Valdes, Gabriola, Lasqueti, Hornby, Denman, Texada and Quadra islands (note that some of these bear Spanish names, the consequence of Spanish exploration in the late eighteenth century). These islands look to Nanaimo as their principal economic centre. Continuing along the inside passage and in a northerly direction one finds a number of other islands. However it can probably rightly be said that most of them are dependencies of the mainland itself. Two in Queen Charlotte Strait—Alert Bay and Malcolm Islands—are definitely oriented towards the communities of Port McNeill and Port Hardy. In the mouth of Queen Charlotte Strait, Hope and Nigel Islands are definitely part of the northern section of Vancouver Island. To the north-east lie Lanz and Cox Islands off Cape Scott; these would undoubtedly represent the extreme limits of island dependence. Any islands beyond them would surely no longer be considered part of greater Vancouver Island, and would, instead, be part of the Queen Charlotte Islands themselves.

On the western side of Vancouver Island are a few islands which, like the general area, are virtually uninhabited. Indeed, the west coast of the main island is very unlike the eastern coast with numerous dependent communities.

Vancouver Island itself is divisible into certain very distinct regions. These are partly geographical and partly the consequence of history. Not everyone would agree with the boundaries of these areas as set out here, but they are convenient groupings. The southern tip of Vancouver Island is dominated by Greater Victoria. The latter's sphere of influence extends over the Saanich Peninsula, over some islands on the eastern coast, and to the west to Sooke, Metchosin, Jordan River and probably to Port Renfrew. The Cowichan Valley and its several small towns are also part of the southern region. A second division is focused on Nanaimo— referred to in the past as 'Victoria's step-daughter'. The Nanaimo sphere of influence runs up the entire eastern coast as far north as Kelsey Bay. The western district is at present the least well developed. Alberni is its chief centre but to some degree this is artificial. To be sure, the only roads leading to Tofino and and Ucluelet on the one hand and Bamfield on the other go from Alberni, but the latter town is itself really part of the central

29

region. The western region is accessible in only a very limited fashion and chiefly by sea and air. The northern district is quite special. A line drawn to the west from Campbell River to include all land north of it—excluding only the narrow coastal lands to Kelsey Bay—would be the best way to delimit this area. There are certain communities, such as the new town of Gold River, which are included in this region but which are not totally dependent on any major centre. Moreover, because much of this area is under lease to the great logging companies and because access is restricted, there is the very real feeling that one is in a different country. The northern communities are separated from the south by closed logging areas—travel on some logging roads is permitted in a limited fashion—and are thereby cut off from the traditional pull towards Nanaimo and Victoria. To emphasise this one only need take cognisance of the fact that residents of such communities as Port Hardy and Port McNeill tend to go more to Vancouver on the mainland. In the past coastal shipping to the north had its headquarters in Vancouver. This tendency has increased over the years—air travel to Vancouver is easier than to Victoria—but when a road is built from Kelsey Bay to Beaver Cove the pattern might be altered.

It is clear that for complete integration of the island regions many and extensive new roads will have to be built. However, these roads are unlikely to be constructed for some years, since the general population of the island does not warrant such a programme. Other parts of British Columbia have a higher priority with the Department of Highways in road construction. Yet, the long term future of Vancouver Island is directly related to an increased population, and this requires better communications.

2   HISTORY

THE earliest history of Vancouver Island is that of prehistoric nomadic tribes. Evidence of their existence is
found particularly in a series of petroglyphs or rock carvings which were done many thousand years ago. Little specific is
known of the peoples who left these records. The best petroglyphs
on the island are preserved in a park just south of Nanaimo. The
figures are carved in the rock; they are of varying sizes—the
largest is about 4ft—and they represent some sort of mythological
beasts. Some have a wolf's head, while others are possibly fish.
Other petroglyphs are found at Sooke, Tofino, at Nitinat and
Sproat Lakes and on the west coast of Clo-oose. Perhaps in some
way they were connected with Aztlan, the legendary home of the
Aztecs. Roderic Cameron in his *Viceroyalties of the West* observes
in a note on page 53 that 'One source claims that Aztlan is Vancouver Island on the North American coast.' Anthropological
and archaeological research seems to indicate that these ancient
peoples were not the immediate ancestors of the native Indian.
The petroglyphs which were discovered by the white man in the
mid-nineteenth century have fascinated and intrigued scholars
since that time.

The native Indian occupied the island for a long time before
it was colonised by the European. The Indians lived a tribal
existence, with each tribe—and these were quite numerous—
dominating a particular geographical area. Warfare between the
tribes was frequent and the fiercest warriors were the Haida.
These Indians lived not only on Vancouver Island, but also in
the Queen Charlotte Islands.

The native population had quite a high level of civilisation,

31

and were not unsophisticated. Their numerous artifacts indicate
an awareness and a cultural perception of real maturity. Their
art forms—particularly their carvings, taking the forms of masks
and totem poles—are very handsome. Many fine examples
remain : some of the best are in the possession of the Provincial
Museum in Victoria. The art of carving has not been lost. Superb
poles and like objects are still being made which compare favour-
ably with earlier examples. Many of the carvings are in wood—
some of the best early art works have disappeared through neg-
lect and decay—but there are carvings in other media as well.

There is a very real indication that there were contacts between
the Orient, the South Pacific and Vancouver Island. However,
no permanent settlements remain to indicate precisely how this
intercommunication operated. Suffice it to say that there is considerable archaeological evidence, such as coins and other artifacts,
to support the thesis that these various civilisations did meet at
various times.

THE AGE OF DISCOVERY

The earlier explorers of the Pacific Ocean do not appear to have
discovered the existence of Vancouver Island. There is, however,
the strange story of one Juan de Fuca who told an Englishman
he met in Italy that he had discovered a broad inlet which, if
followed to its head, would open up the hinterland of the continent. De Fuca claimed to have made his discoveries in 1592, a
century after Columbus, and while he was in the employ of the
Spanish governor of Mexico. How much credence contemporaries
gave to his story is an open question. Certainly later explorers
dismissed his tale as entirely fictitious. De Fuca remains a man
of mystery; certainly no inlet existed precisely where he said it
ought to be.

During the eighteenth century the Spaniards slowly expanded
their knowledge of the western shores of North America. Juan
Perez sailed from Mexico in 1774 and actually sighted the Queen
Charlotte Islands. He also lay off Estevan Point on the entrance

to Nootka Sound. The Indians were amazed when they first saw his ship and a few hardy souls probably came alongside for a closer look. Perez very likely gave them the usual presents reserved for such occasions. It was Perez's intention to land, but bad weather prevented him. Had he gone ashore he would have been the first white man to land on Vancouver Island.

Contemporaneous with Spanish exploration, the Russians, too, were active in the northern Pacific off Alaska, later to become their colony. As a result the Russians were to lay claim to all of the territory as far south as northern California. The claims conflicted with those of the Spanish, who based their rights on treaties and pronouncements of the sixteenth century.

The year 1776 not only saw the American *Declaration of Independence* and Adam Smith's *The Wealth of Nations*—both in their way important to the development of Vancouver Island —but also it was the year that Captain James Cook set sail from England. On 12 July 1776, when the *Discovery* and the *Resolution* weighed anchor, their commander's hope was to discover the northwest passage. The stakes were high, for if such a route were found the age-old longing for an easy route to the Far East would have become a reality. To show how important they felt such a discovery would be, the authorities had put up £20,000 as a prize.

Cook slowly made his way to the western coast off North America and sailed steadily into the upper reaches of the Pacific. He knew of de Fuca's claims; accordingly, when he actually was off the shore of western North America in the region of 47° and 48° latitude where the inlet was presumed to exist, he kept a sharp look out. He found no sign of de Fuca's waterway. He observed, 'saw nothing like it; nor is there the least possibility that any such thing ever existed'.

On 29 March 1778 Cook discovered Nootka Sound. He anchored in Friendly Cove, which became the basis for future English claims. When James Cook arrived he was received in a most cordial fashion by Chief Maquinna and his fellow Indians. The natives offered otter skins and other pelts in exchange for items aboard the British ships.

Cook's journals are filled with interesting comments about the Indians. He took notes on their activities and their culture. He understood from what was said to him that the indigenous people were cannibals. This was really not true, and may have been put about in order to make the Indians seem even more fierce.

The English ships remained in Friendly Cove for about a month. During their stay the crews had acquired many excellent furs at a low cost. They paid about sixpence a pelt for otters which they were to sell later at over one thousand per cent profit. The *Resolution* and the *Discovery*, after leaving Nootka, made their way to Macao and ultimately back to England. On a later expedition, exploring the Pacific Ocean, Cook was killed when visiting the Sandwich Islands.

Following Captain Cook's successful visit and the reports of the potential value of the fur trade, interest in the area increased considerably. Nootka was to become a real centre of trade. James Hanna was the first of a series of traders to take advantage of the contact with the Indians. When Hanna arrived in 1785 his reception was somewhat mixed; indeed, the Indians actually made an attempt to seize his ship. They were not successful. However, Hanna apparently bore them little ill-will for their behaviour. He was very probably not overly surprised—contact with native populations everywhere was always somewhat hazardous. Hanna had not hesitated to use his cannon and other armaments against the Indians when they attacked him. Thereafter, the Indians had a healthy respect for the white trader.

In 1786 two more vessels, the *Captain Cook* and the *Experiment*, were both actively involved in trade with the Indians. When they departed John Mackay, the surgeon, remained at Nootka; he was ill and thus disinclined to make the long voyage. Moreover, both he and James Strange, who had organised the expedition, wished to know more about the Indians. Strange consequently approved of Mackay's plan; he probably felt that future trade would be increased as a result. With any luck Mackay would be able to persuade the Indians to save their best furs for him. Therefore, when the *Captain Cook* and the *Experi-*

34

Page 35 (above) Nootka Sound on the west coast of the island is still virtually as it was when Captain Cook landed in the late eighteenth century; (below) the growing of small fruits such as loganberries, raspberries, blackberries, is an important aspect of agricultural life on the island

Page 36 *(above)* Bulbs and seeds grown in Saanich form a significant part of the economic life of the farmer; *(below)* so large are the modern machines used in the woods that men are almost midgets beside them

ment sailed they left behind the first white man to settle on Vancouver Island.

The next year Charles Barkley, accompanied by his young wife, reached Nootka on board the *Imperial Eagle*. Mrs Barkley was the first white woman to reach Vancouver Island. She kept a journal in which she recounted her adventures. Many of her experiences were quite astounding and must have seemed truly fantastic. The way of life and the attitudes of the Indians were far removed from the world she had known in England.

John Mackay was very glad to see Barkley. He had found that native life was far from agreeable. Moreover, the Indians, tiring of having him in their midst, treated him somewhat roughly. By the time Barkley encountered him Mackay was thoroughly disenchanted with his existence. His physical state had deteriorated —he was much emaciated—and he looked like a poor native. Barkley took him aboard the *Imperial Eagle*; the first white inhabitant of Vancouver Island was glad to be with his own kind once again.

Barkley left Nootka and sailed in a southerly direction. He made his way along the western coast of the island and found a body of water which seemed to confirm de Fuca's earlier claims. In recognition of this, Barkley named his discovery the Strait of Juan de Fuca.

When James Meares arrived at Nootka on 13 May 1788 he received a particularly cordial reception from Chief Maquinna. The particular reason for the chief's friendliness was that Comekala, his brother, was a passenger on Meares's ship, the *Felice Adventurer*. Comekala had some time before gone off on one of the trading vessels, and, having been abandoned in China, was at a loss how to get back to Nootka. Meares found him and restored him to his family. Maquinna was much pleased to see his brother again—the latter was all decked out in a red coat and gay apparel for the meeting.

Naturally, Meares's stock was very high; he decided to take advantage of the situation to acquire land and erect a permanent building. Maquinna agreed to sell him some land, and Meares put up a two-storey structure. At the same time he and his men built a schooner which was christened *North-West-America* and which was launched later in the summer of 1788. This was the first vessel, excepting Indian canoes, built on Vancouver Island. The *North-West-America* was not very large—something under 50 tons burden—but she was a good ship, very seaworthy, and was later to chart part of the coast on Queen Charlotte Sound.

The British trading activities were not destined to continue for long unhampered. Don Estevan Martinez sailed into Nootka Sound on 5 May 1789. At once he proceeded to declare all of the territory part of the dominion of the king of Spain. He arrested Meares and later three other British captains, and accused them of violating Spanish decrees. Several American ships were also anchored in the harbour, but they were not molested. The news of Martinez's activities was reported to his home government. The Spaniards proceeded to press their claims to all of the lands and trading rights, thereby outraging the British.

Instead of agreeing to Madrid's demands, the British proceeded to put forth counter-claims. The British government demanded an apology from Spain for the presumptuous behaviour of Martinez; further, it insisted that all of the men held as prisoners be released at once, that the ships be restored to their captains, and that the owners be recompensed for their loss of trade. The Spanish government declined to accept the demands as put forth in the British ultimatum, and war seemed the inevitable result. However, the Spaniards discovered that they could not rely on 'the Family Compact'—the Franco-Spanish alliance made earlier in the century—because the French were too involved in their own domestic affairs as a result of the outbreak of the revolution. Without help from Paris the government in Madrid did not dare to risk a conflict with Great Britain. Therefore, the Spanish authorities decided to enter into negotiations with the British. The latter's demands were accepted in 'the Nootka Convention'.

While the chanceries in London and Madrid were busily engaged in the war of despatches, the Spaniards were firmly establishing themselves at Nootka. They constructed a number of buildings and created a real settlement. They also organised further exploratory expeditions. Manuel Quimper sailed into the Strait of Juan de Fuca and discovered Sooke Inlet, Esquimalt and the inner harbour of Victoria. Other Spaniards, such as Eliza and Narvaez, made voyages along the eastern side of Vancouver Island.

At long last the British government ordered Captain George Vancouver and HMS *Discovery* to depart for western North America. He reached his destination in the spring of 1792. Instead of proceeding directly to Nootka to carry out the terms of the convention of 1790, he rounded Cape Flattery, sailed down the Strait of Juan de Fuca, rounded the southern tip of the island and then went north through the Strait of Georgia. During his northerly tour of exploration he met two Spanish captains, Galiano and Valdez. After greeting his fellow explorers in a friendly fashion, he continued on his way charting and naming various points and islands. Finally he reached Nootka on 12 August 1792, and here he met Bodega y Quadra. Relations between the two officers were most cordial. Vancouver chose to emphasise this in a very special fashion. He proceeded to name the island he had just circumnavigated Quadra's and Vancouver's Island.

As a result of George Vancouver's arrival the terms of the treaty could now be put into effect. However, it was not until three years later that the denouement occurred. In 1795 the Spanish flag was lowered, the British flag was unfurled, and after further ceremonies the entire establishment at Nootka was formally abandoned by both parties. The initial attempts at permanent settlement were at an end.

Although no European community existed, trade with Maquinna and his tribesmen continued. The Indians now seemed courteous enough, but it is evident that they intended to take advantage of anything that might arise. Moreover, the traders were not always overly polite to Maquinna, and this did not really inspire confidence. Therefore, when in 1803 Maquinna and his Indians captured the American vessel, the *Boston*, and killed the captain and all but two of the crew, it was not altogether surprising.

Maquinna took the two crewmen, John Jewitt and John Thompson, who survived and made them his slaves. Their existence became very grim. They were held in slavery for a couple of years and were only released through trickery. The Indian chief himself was held as a hostage on the *Lydia*, another American ship, after he had gone aboard on a visit. Maquinna had carried a letter from Jewitt to the captain of the *Lydia;* the chief thought the letter commended his activities, but in fact was a plea for help. The captain of the *Lydia* would only release the Indian if Jewitt and Thompson were freed. This was agreed to; however, Maquinna was very sorry to see his two slaves depart. Although he had treated them somewhat roughly, he seemed to have developed an affection for them as well, and he wept as he bade them adieu.

THE DAYS OF THE COMPANY

Permanent settlement of Vancouver Island was the direct consequence of the Oregon Boundary question. When it became clear that much, if not all, of the Oregon territory was to become American, the Hudson's Bay Company wished to have its western headquarters on British soil. In 1842 James Douglas, the Chief Factor for the company, left Fort Nisqually aboard the schooner *Cadboro*. He intended to make a tour of Southern Vancouver Island to find a suitable spot to establish a new post. He chose the 'Port of Camosack'; he rejected Esquimalt although it had a much better harbour, because the surrounding terrain was rocky and not particularly agreeable. 'Camosack' had great charm, with meadows and oaks—almost as if it were a gentleman's country domain.

Once the site was selected, Douglas gave the necessary commands for the construction of essential buildings. The result was Fort Camosun. The stockade was 300ft by 350ft in area with defensive palings of 18ft. There were eight buildings in all.

Roderick Finlayson, an employee of the company, was left in charge. A Roman Catholic priest, Father Bolduc, who had accompanied Douglas in his initial tour of exploration, settled himself at the new Hudson's Bay Company port. The priest's missionary work with the local Indians was quite successful, and he soon made a number of converts.

The name Fort Camosun did not long remain the official designation of the new post. Suggestions were made initially that it should be called Fort Albert—in honour of the husband of the queen—but then the authorities settled upon the name of Fort Victoria. There were no real settlers as such, but only employees of the company. However, by 1846 some 160 acres were cleared. Three years later Fort Victoria officially became the western coastal headquarters of the Hudson's Bay Company.

Vancouver Island formally became a crown colony in 1849. At this time the entire island belonged to the company. Settlers were encouraged to come to the island and buy land at £1 per acre. With land at such a high price, it was felt that only settlers of real substance would be able to come to the colony, thereby preventing undesirables from taking up land. As a further limitation of settlement, the company had a complete monopoly on all trade. This meant that all goods and services were quite expensive. Individuals with little ready money were really excluded from the colony.

The consequence of the extremely expensive land prices and the high cost of living was that nobody came at all. The company at this stage was doing little to encourage any but its own people. The first officially independent settler was Captain Walter Colquhoun Grant. He arrived in June 1849. He brought with him some employees and acquired 200 acres in Sooke, near Fort Victoria. However, even he was not totally free of the company, for he was to do some surveying for them. Regretfully, as a settler he did not prosper : he attempted to live in the style of the landed gentleman in an environment that was unsuitable. He gave up the experiment in a few years and returned home to Great Britain. One of his men, John Muir, bought the farm.

With the formal creation of Vancouver Island as a crown colony, it was necessary to set up an administration, and this meant that a governor had to be appointed. The chief executive at this stage should have been James Douglas, but the authorities chose to appoint an outsider. Richard Blanshard arrived on 10 March 1850. He found nothing prepared for him. He was treated somewhat scurvily by the company, who had made certain promises which were not kept. For example, the cost of his trip was about £300; the company reimbursed him to the sum of £175 only, instead of paying it in full. Moreover, Blanshard had been promised some land for himself in the colony, but he never received any such grant. When he arrived he found that he had no house and no establishment; the real authority was Douglas, the chief factor.

Richard Blanshard was no fool. He was a man of considerable perceptivity, and he wrote some excellent reports on the island and its future needs. He remained in office for a little over a year; he actually resigned in November 1850, but stayed on the island colony until the following summer, finally leaving on 1 September 1851. Prior to his departure he appointed a small council, and one of its members was James Douglas. In November 1851 the Crown named the latter as the new chief executive. With him at the helm, the colony really began to develop.

It may be truly said that James Douglas is the father of Vancouver Island as it now exists. He was born in the West Indies, joined the Hudson's Bay Company at an early age, and, in due course, was sent to the west coast where he ultimately became the chief factor. As a man he loved order and gave much deference to the ways of convention. He was, as R. E. Gosnell, an earlier historian, noted, 'a strong masterful man with the faults such men have—the tendency to rule with too firm a hand, to brook no opposition, to be perhaps too overbearing'. He 'possessed the quality of personal magnetism in a high degree . . . cool, calculating and cautious. . . '. All his life he seemed to know exactly what he was doing.

From 1851 to 1856 Governor Douglas and the little council

administered the colony. Settlers slowly began to take up land, and create a real colonial society. Money was raised for revenue, roads and schools were built and local JPs were appointed.

Progress was slow; the population was still small. During the Crimean War there was a fear that the Russians might launch an attack from Alaska on the little colony. A local rifle company was formed by way of protection and a small naval hospital was built at Esquimalt, for already the navy was making regular calls and by 1865 it had created a permanent shore establishment. This base at Esquimalt remained under the control of the Admiralty in Whitehall until 1905.

The first elected assembly of the colony met in 1856. It had seven members. The opening ceremonies had all the formality, albeit on a miniature scale, of Westminster. This little legislative body continued until 1859, when the Hudson's Bay Company's control was terminated.

Colonial society was very circumscribed. The principal figures were either company men or near relations of Governor Douglas. For example, the speaker of the assembly, Helmcken, was the governor's son-in-law and the chief justice, Cameron—who incidentally was not even a lawyer—was Douglas's brother-in-law. Naturally, anyone who was outside the charmed circle was likely to be somewhat hostile. With the arrival of Amor De Cosmos in 1858, the anti-establishment party gained a real leader. He founded a newspaper, *The British Colonist*, as a rival to the semi-official *Victoria Gazette*. De Cosmos regarded Douglas as a tyrant and he opposed him constantly. 'Old square-toes', as the governor was nick-named, attempted to silence his opponents, but with only limited success.

The decision to end company control meant that some changes were inevitable. The chief one was that the company gave up its rights and land monopoly for £57,000. Douglas was permitted to continue as governor, but he had to end his association with the company. The second phase of development of the island colony was about to begin.

During the period of company control on the island the main-

43

land also began to become settled. In 1858 Queen Victoria formally approved the change of name of the sister colonial territory in western North America from New Caledonia to British Columbia. In a letter dated 24 July 1858, Her Majesty wrote as follows :

> If the name New Caledonia is objected to as being borne by another colony or island claimed by the French, it may be better to give the new colony west of the Rocky Mountains another name. . . . The only name which is given to the whole territory in every map the Queen has consulted is 'Columbia' but as there exists also a Columbia in South America, and the citizens of the United States call their country also Columbia, at least in poetry, 'British Columbia' might be, in the Queen's opinion, the best name.

COLONIAL LIFE

With the gold rush British Columbia experienced a vast influx of settlers, many of them Americans. In order to establish British authority firmly and to maintain public order Douglas took over the administration of British Columbia as well. Victoria became the centre of considerable importance—particularly as a place for miners to acquire their supplies before going on to seek their fortunes on the mainland.

Douglas continued his tandem administration until 1863. In that year he gave up his post as governor of Vancouver Island and the next year retired as chief executive of British Columbia. The two colonies were formally united in 1866. Sir James Douglas —he had been knighted prior to his retirement—did not favour colonial union. He noted in his daughter's journal of 19 November 1866, 'The Ships of War fired a salute on the occasion—a funeral procession, with minute guns would have been more appropriate to the sad melancholy event.'

During the long period of Douglas's governmental services other areas of the island began to be settled. The governor acquired all of Saanich—some 50,000 acres—from the Indians in 1852 for the paltry sum of £177 1s. 8d. This was followed by a number of

44

individuals taking up land for farming. In addition, Saltspring Island just off Sidney had applications from potential settlers in 1859. Many of the earliest settlers on Saltspring Island were Negroes who had emigrated from the United States. Slightly earlier, Captain Edward Langford, his wife and daughters had settled on a farm at Colwood. It was here in 1853 that his son, George Langford, the first white child, was born. In the late 1850s a few farms were to be found in the Cowichan Valley and Father Rondeault had set up a mission in the Indian village of Comiaken where he built his first church. He later erected a stone building, known as 'The Butter Church', since he paid some of his labourers with butter. This edifice was 64ft long, 30ft wide and 30ft high at the gable ends. It was abandoned after a decade of service but still stands, having been repaired in 1967

The discovery of coal at the north end of the island, at Beaver Harbour, in 1835 resulted ultimately in a small settlement at Fort Rupert. The mines, however, were not very productive, and the miners were somewhat discontented with the general treatment they received from the company. The discovery of coal near Nanaimo somewhat later provided a more lasting community. The company built a small fort or garrison centre at Nanaimo in 1853.

The Indians provided excitement from time to time. At an early stage of settlement Fort Camosun itself was attacked. Periodically, a white man was murdered and the authorities had to show their power. For example, in 1852 a shepherd named Peter Brown was killed. The culprits fled, Douglas and his posse went after them; the Indians were caught, tried aboard the *Beaver* and hanged. The trial and execution were all over in about one hour.

Chief Tzouhalem of the Comiaken tribe raided a number of other Indian communities and he, too, lay seige to Fort Victoria. Tzouhalem's chief concern was in the maintenance of his power over his fellow Indians, and the whites were rarely in real danger. Tzouhalem was killed when he attempted to abduct a new wife from Kuper Island. The irate husband of the lady in question trapped Tzouhalem and cut off his head. His death was unla-

45

mented. There is a story that after his death Tzouhalem's heart was removed from his body to find out why he had been such an evil man. His unpleasant character was apparently the result of having a heart no larger than that of a salmon.

A more amusing incident occurred at Fort Rupert when the Indians 'borrowed' James Dunsmuir, who was the first white child they had ever seen. After frantic searchings by his parents and their friends, the infant turned up quite unharmed in a near-by Indian village. He had been abducted as a sort of curiosity and was none the worse for his experiences, but his parents kept a close eye on him to prevent a second disappearance.

Life on Vancouver Island was not unlike that of British colonial society everywhere. Class structure was somewhat rigid. Englishmen were more acceptable than immigrants from elsewhere. Lawyers, for example, who were members of the British bar could practise at once in the colony; lawyers from other places, including other British North American colonies, were generally not so fortunate.

Government House was the centre of social life. Douglas and his successors, as the sovereign's representatives, were generally quite lavish in their hospitality. Balls were given when the navy made its periodic visits. Amateur theatricals were popular in winter and picnics in summer. The masonic lodges which were established quite early were much favoured by the business community. Debating and literary associations had considerable support from all segments of society. There were horse-races and similar sporting events. Life on the island was simple but not dull.

With the union of the colonies of Vancouver Island and British Columbia in 1866 the town of New Westminster was declared the colonial capital. Victoria was somewhat like the abandoned maiden, the heroine of many a nineteenth-century novel. However, her citizens did not give up all hope; after much debate, Victoria became the centre of administration anew in 1868. There was great joy among the islanders when the decision was announced, for there was a very real rivalry between the island and the mainland.

UNION WITH CANADA

With the formation of the Dominion of Canada in 1867, the impetus for a union between the newly-created nation and the western colony increased. However, the 'confederationists' discovered that the people on Vancouver Island were less enthusiastic than some of their mainland friends. Amor De Cosmos, the leading figure in favour of confederation, used all of his talents to encourage it. In the summer of 1871 British Columbia became a province of Canada, and Victoria was designated the provincial capital.

In the years immediately following confederation, public attention on the island was focused on two principal issues. The first was over the construction of a graving dock at Esquimalt. This was promised under the 'terms of union'. It was initially begun in 1874, but progress was extremely slow. It was not completed until a decade after work had begun. When it was opened it provided repair facilities not only for coastal and trans-Pacific shipping but for the Royal Navy as well. During World War II one of the many ships repaired in the graving dock was the *Queen Elizabeth*. The second great issue involved the island and the railway. To nineteenth-century people the railway was a talisman promising prosperity and happiness. The government in Ottawa had promised a trans-continental railway as part of the terms of union. Residents of Vancouver Island hoped that this railway would be so constructed that, by bridging Seymour Narrows, Esquimalt would be the western terminus. Such a plan was not followed; instead, first Port Moody and then later Vancouver was the end of the Canadian Pacific Railway. The islanders naturally felt very aggrieved. They had to be content with a boat service from the mainland.

Even so, they still wanted their own railway. After considerable negotiations, Robert Dunsmuir, the coal magnate, and some others organised the building of the Esquimalt and Nanaimo Railway. It was completed in 1886 at a cost of $750,000·00 (£300,000).* The last spike was driven on 13 August near

* For convenience of conversion, £1 is approximately equal to $2·50 (Canadian).

Shawnigan by Sir John A. Macdonald, the first prime minister of Canada. The new railway opened up much of the central part of the island. In 1914 the line was extended to Courtenay, a distance of about 50 miles. The Esquimalt and Nanaimo Railway was later acquired by the Canadian Pacific. A second line was built as part of the Canadian Northern Pacific; it was finally amalgamated with the Canadian National Railway. Several minor passenger and freight railways were constructed by private entrepreneurs, but these did not long survive. The logging industry used trains and laid extensive lines of tracks in the woods to transport equipment and timber.

From 1871 to 1886 representation in the provincial legislature favoured Vancouver Island. The latter sent twelve members to the house, while the much larger mainland elected only thirteen. Redistribution was inevitable. By the end of the nineteenth century proper representation by population had been achieved. However, this meant that the island's influence was increasingly less in the development of British Columbia.

The residents of New Westminster had never forgotten that for a brief time their town had been the colonial capital. Periodically there was agitation to move the centre of administration back to the mainland from the island. Whether anyone seriously considered it feasible is an open question, but people were still somewhat emotional on the issue. The matter was finally and irrevocably concluded when the provincial government under Premier Theodore Davie authorised the construction of new legislative buildings to replace the old 'birdcages'; these new government buildings were in Victoria.

The provincial legislature buildings were designed by F. M. Rattenbury. They were very much of the age of empire—somewhat grandiose, not unlike a rajah's palace, with a stone exterior and miles of corridors decorated with marble. They were completed in 1897 and with their formal opening the capital was firmly secured on the island.

Although the population of the island was some 36,000 by 1891, it was heavily concentrated in a few specific areas. Much of the island still remained relatively unknown. Therefore, in 1894 an expedition under the leadership of the Reverend W. W. Bolton was organised to explore those parts which had not been previously visited by white man. There had been a similar sort of expedition thirty years earlier. Both expeditions concentrated on the north and north-west. A good deal of information on the area was collected, but settlers were not greatly attracted since the terrain explored was relatively inaccessible. However, by 1897 Quatsino had been settled by Norwegians and Cape Scott by Danes.

The need for an increased population led the provincial government to advertise widely. Many of the statements put out did much to publicise the sporting and agricultural potentialities of British Columbia. Of course, Vancouver Island was included in these advertisements. The Cowichan Valley was stated to be a sportsman's paradise, with fishing and shooting to satisfy the most ardent Nimrod.

Quite a number of English families settled in and around Duncan. This community soon acquired the sobriquet 'a little bit of olde England'. A way of life was established that was to be unique, with games of all sorts—tennis, cricket, polo and rugby; afternoon tea as a daily ritual; dances—young ladies 'came out in Duncan'. A sort of late Victorian country life spread and flourished. Other communities in the environs of Duncan were similar. For example, Maple Bay was very select indeed. It was said somewhat facetiously that if one shouted 'Colonel!' every other man in the district would turn round. The settlers bore the surnames of some of the most distinguished families in Great Britain. This very special world suffered a mortal blow with the outbreak of the war in 1914. All of the fit young men volunteered—some joined the Canadian forces, while others crossed the Atlantic to become part of the British army—and a glance at the war memorial in St Peter's Church at Quamichan indicates how many failed to return. In the years between 1918 and 1939 the English way of life continued, but it was kept alive by an older generation.

Vancouver Island, from the death of Queen Victoria to 1914, shared in the general prosperity of Canada. However, there were a number of strikes, particularly in the coal mining industry. General communications improved; there was increased coastal shipping, the cable and wireless had a station at Bamfield, electric trams came to Victoria, the rich began to acquire motor cars and the electric power line was found in rural communities. Sir Richard McBride, the youthful and handsome provincial premier, embodied the optimism of the age.

To promote domestic science and rural life generally, the first Women's Institute in British Columbia was organised in Metchosin in 1909. (Women's Institutes had been founded in Ontario in 1897.) One of the original members was Mrs Alfred Watt. Four years later she returned to England—her husband Dr Watt had died in the meantime—and settled there. For the next few years she actually promoted the idea of Women's Institutes in lectures all over Great Britain. In 1915 the first of the Women's Institutes was organised in Wales. From that time on the movement became widespread. Thus, a little gathering at Metchosin on Vancouver Island was to affect the lives of English, Welsh and Scottish women to our own day. Mrs Watt continued to be associated with the Women's Institutes on both sides of the Atlantic until her death in 1948.

FROM WORLD WAR I THROUGH WORLD WAR II

When Canada declared war against Germany in August 1914, many residents of the island joined the colours. The civilian population threw themselves into war work. The coal miners, some of whom had been on strike for quite a time, returned to the mines. The initial enthusiasm for the war inevitably lessened with the failure to attain military victory. Popular disenchantment finally erupted following the news of the sinking of the *Lusitania*. At the same time there were rumours that Mrs Barnard, who was of German extraction and the wife of the lieutenant-governor, had celebrated the kaiser's birthday. There were also reports

50

that members of the German community had been sending signals out to sea. The consequence was a major riot in Victoria. A local brewery was set on fire and there was a march on Government House. Troops had to be called out to restore order and for a time the situation was extremely unpleasant. In the end nobody was killed, but there were some injuries.

Following the signing of the armistice in 1918 there was a recession which lasted until 1921. From that time until the market crash in 1929, the happy pre-war existence seems to have returned. The population continued to increase—in the decade 1921 to 1931 it went up from 108,792 to 120,933. Logging, fishing and mining were expanded and agriculture held its own.

However, Vancouver Island did not escape the effects of the depression. Many men were thrown out of work as the markets for raw materials like timber dried up. The number of ships calling at the various ports fell to almost none. The effects of the depression were probably less severe than in large urban communities. Even so, places such as Nanaimo, Comox and Ladysmith became depressed areas.

There was little to cheer the islanders in the 1930s; the economic situation scarcely improved and general world conditions were gloomy. In spite of all this, the residents of the island were enthusiastic in the welcome they gave to King George VI and Queen Elizabeth in 1939. This was the first time that the reigning monarch had come to Vancouver Island. Old loyalties and sentiments were revived; historic ties were renewed. Indeed, it may well be that this was the last time that the idea of empire had real viability. Of course, there had been previous royal visitors— in the nineteenth century the Princess Louise had accompanied her husband, the Marquess of Lorne, when he served as governor-general; at the turn of the century a brief call was made by the Duke and Duchess of York—afterwards King George V and Queen Mary; later there were visits by the Duke of Connaught, and in the 1920s the Prince of Wales and his brother, the Duke of Kent, had come to the island. However, the royal visit in 1939

51

had a special significance, and more so when it was so closely followed by war.

The 1939–45 war marked the close of yet another phase of the island's history. After the war the old patterns were completely gone, and also the residents began to see themselves more as Canadians; 'home' was the island and not the British Isles. During the war the naval base at Esquimalt was greatly enlarged; the need for timber, minerals, fish and agricultural produce to help the war effort revitalised the economy; and, as in 1914, many young people—both men and women—entered the armed forces. Vancouver Island's patriotism was as strong in the second war as in the first.

Following the Japanese attack on Pearl Harbour in 1941 Vancouver Island had the peculiar distinction of being the only part of Canada to be shelled by the enemy in the Pacific. A submarine bombarded the lighthouse at Estevan Point in June 1941. Following a decision made in Ottawa, the Japanese, who were settled on Vancouver Island and elsewhere in British Columbia, were ordered to leave and to take up residence in the interior of Canada.

THE CONTEMPORARY SCENE

In the post-war years the island truly entered the modern age. Air Canada increased its services and various small independent air lines began to fly to the more isolated areas. The ferry service to the mainland was vastly improved—there was a concommitant decline in the services of the Canadian Pacific coastal shipping. New pulp mills were built at Crofton and Harmoc, while earlier ones at Port Alice and Alberni were enlarged. The government created 'instant' towns at Gold River—this was to be the community for a new pulp mill—and Rumble Beach. While the coal industry declined with the increase of hydro-electric power, other mines such as copper and molybdenum began to expand.

Many new roads were constructed : the north-south highway, 'the Malahat', was vastly modernised, being widened and resur-

Page 53 (above) After the logger has done his work, the area looks devastated but in a few years the hills are soon covered with young seedling trees; (below) the pulp mill at Port Alice was the first to be constructed on the island to use the sulphite process

Page 54 (above) Tourism is a major industry and all tastes are catered for. The Empress Hotel in Victoria is one of the most famous hostelries in North America; *(below)* the 'lodge' is very much part of Canadian life and it provides first-class service and comfort in a rustic setting. Eaglecrest Lodge is one of the best examples of such places

faced; the east-west road from Alberni to Tofino and Ucluelet ceased to be exclusively a logging road and was no longer just a gravel track; the road from Campbell River to Kelsey Bay was completed, and there were plans to construct the final piece of roadway to Port McNeill.

The island finally acquired its own university in 1963. However, since before World War I there had been an affiliated college which was part of the University of British Columbia. Other institutions of higher learning, such as Malaspina College at Nanaimo, were organised by the provincial and civic authorities.

In the centennial year of Canadian Confederation, 1967, Vancouver Island joined in the celebrations. A much more elaborate birthday was celebrated in 1971, the one hundredth anniversary of the union of British Columbia with Canada. A very special aspect of these centennial celebrations was the visit of Queen Elizabeth accompanied by Prince Philip and Princess Anne. The royal party made an extended tour of British Columbia including Vancouver Island. As in the past the royal visitors were received in Victoria at Government House as guests of the province.

By the mid-sixties the population had reached 333,951. About one half, viz, 147,312, lived in the metropolitan district of Greater Victoria; the rest of the population divided into the following divisions : 167,096 resided in the area between Victoria and Campbell River, while the northern section had 19,543. The population has continued to increase, with immigrants from all over the world as well as many people from the rest of Canada settling on Vancouver Island. It is a far cry from the tiny communities established by the Spaniards at Nootka and the Hudson's Bay Company at the 'Port of Camosack'.

The future history of Vancouver Island is inextricably bound up with the story of Canada. The islanders are proud of their past; they maintain a friendly rivalry with their fellow British Columbians on the mainland, but, although they may be islanders first, whatever their ethnic or natural origin, they are also true Canadians.

D

3　　　THE ECONOMY—a mosaic

AGRICULTURE

FOLLOWING the erection of Fort Victoria, land was cleared for agricultural use. Within a very few years 160 acres were under cultivation, and by the mid-1850s a subsidiary of Hudson's Bay Company, called the Puget Sound Agricultural Company ran, four largish farms, namely, North Dairy Farm, Colwood Farm, Craigflower Farm and Uplands Farm. Following increased settlement in the Cowichan River Valley during the next decade, more and more land was cleared for agricultural purposes. Since much of the land was heavily forested the settler had no very easy task. Logging, therefore, often had to precede agriculture in general community development.

There were 779 farms listed in the census of 1881. Farming as a way of life continued to attract settlers to the island, but the proportion of the population involved directly in agriculture was to decline relatively, and rapidly, in the twentieth century. Vancouver Island was to be no exception to similar trends in North America.

Although the total area of the island is 8,451,840 acres, a very small proportion only is directly concerned with agriculture. According to a recent census report (1966), 132,305 acres are reckoned to be agricultural land. Of this, some 77,079 are unimproved, ie, 42,844 acres of woodland and 34,235 acres of sloughs, lakes, sand-dunes and rough pasture. This means that only 55,226 acres can be considered as improved land. Of this area some 26,560 acres are under crops; 21,839 are in pasture, and the remaining 6,872 acres, although improved, are not under cultivation.

The total number of farms is correspondingly small, namely,

1,948; of these, 475 are less than 10 acres; 836 are less than 70 acres; 536 less than 1,600 acres, and only one is over 1,600 acres. Moreover, something like 651 of the total number of farms have less than 7 acres under crops. Improved pasture is found on 1,082 farms; again the small areas of the farms should be noted, since more than 65 per cent of them have less than 17 acres of pasture, and only something like 1 per cent of the total have improved pasture over 128 acres. All of this is brought into greater relief when population numbers are given. The total population of the island is something in the order of 335,000, while rather less than 10,000 live on farms.

Of the 1,948 farms in 1966, 1,009 were operated by individuals who worked seventy-five or more days in other jobs or had $750·00 (£300) income from other sources. Yet, most of the persons involved with agricultural activity lived on the farm itself and only a tiny minority—about fifty-four in all—did not reside on the farms which they operated. It is clear from these figures that farming is obviously only a part-time activity and not the major source of livelihood. Indeed, 606 produce below $250·00 (£100) per annum and only 230 gross between $10,000·00 (£4,000) and $25,000·00 (£10,000).

Hay is by far the largest single crop produced, with some 17,696 acres used for this purpose. The next largest crop, but well below the acreage for hay, is approximately 2,337 acres for fodder oats; then there are about 1,414 used to grow fodder crops generally; finally 1,078 acres produce grain oats and 1,063 acres potatoes. All other crops, such as vegetables, small fruits, nursery plants, bulbs and the like are grown on a very small total acreage indeed.

The market for these crops is almost entirely local. The large hay crop is consumed by the livestock on the island. Moreover, even with this quantity of hay other fodder must be trans-shipped from the mainland to support the total agricultural endeavours. The potatoes, other vegetables and small fruits have a ready market in the Greater Victoria area, but the nursery plants, bulbs, flowers—and in particular daffodils—are also sold in large quan-

57

tities on the mainland. It is reported that at Easter over a million dozen daffodils are flown to eastern Canada. Of this number something like 850,000 dozen come from one grower, the Vantreight farms. This same producer exports 150,000 dozen tulips and 30,000 dozen irises.

Of the 619 farms officially rated as commercial, the breakdown is as follows: 195 dairy farms, 115 poultry, 84 livestock, 63 fruit and vegetable, 24 field crops, 8 mixed. There is also a final category of 117 miscellaneous which would include bulb and flower growers. Most of the dairy and poultry products are sold locally, although in peak periods there is some shipment of these to the mainland. Conversely, in periods of low production, the islanders have to depend on the mainland, particularly the Fraser Valley, for milk and eggs.

Despite the relatively small acreage, the livestock numbers are substantial. There are 6,000 veal calves and 4,250 feeder cattle available for market, with 8,000 lambs—on Vancouver Island nobody ever seems to consume mutton—and 6,000 pigs. The amount of livestock might well be increased were it not for the fact that foodstuffs would then have to be brought over to the island.

It is clear from the foregoing that the island at present is not self-sufficient, and it is unlikely to become so in the near future. Agricultural activities have not been greatly expanded in recent years. This is partially the result of limited land which can be considered to have first-class soil. It is reckoned that there are 83,000 acres in this category, 87,000 acres in a secondary classification and 253,000 in a third. However, much of this land is unavailable for agricultural uses; some is still forested and some part of urban areas. In addition, it is relatively expensive, eg, land close to an urban community can sell for $2,000·00 (£800) per acre, while land elsewhere often costs $1,000·00 (£400) per acre. A good stock farm—and this includes land, buildings and stock—sells for $100,000·00 (£40,000) and a fruit and vegetable farm for $50,000·00 (£20,000). The capital outlay is considerable, and equivalent sums of money invested in the stock market today probably bring in a greater return.

FISHING

As could be readily assumed, fishing is very much a major part of the general economic life of the island. Fishing boats of varying sizes and types operate from most of the coastal communities. Two types of fishing vessels are normal; the first is the trawler, which concentrates its effort on the taking of spring and coho salmon; the second is the netter—the grill and the sein—which catches sockeye, pink chum and coho salmon. Both trawlers and netters catch other fish as well, depending upon the season. Something in the order of 4,000 men and 3,000 boats are actively involved in the commercial fishing industry.

The salmon catch is concentrated during the months from June to the end of September. Only spring salmon are caught for commercial purposes during the winter months and even these on a fairly limited scale. The total annual salmon catch—commercial only—for 1969 was as follows: spring 70,898cwt, sockeye 81,697cwt, coho 102,741cwt, pinks 74,273cwt and chum 58,686cwt. There are two salmon canneries in operation on the island, and there are also cold storage facilities in several of the coastal towns.

In addition to the large salmon catch, other fish are taken as well. Steelhead—a sort of sea-going rainbow trout—are treated like salmon, ie, caught in the net or on the line, and a few hundredweight each year are tinned, while others are sold directly in the fish markets. The halibut catch is quite considerable, caught chiefly in spring and summer by long-line, but it is not overly profitable. Prices per pound to the fisherman are low. As the annual *Report* of the Department of Recreation and Conservation observed, this is because of 'a large flounder masquerading on the market as (Greenland) halibut'. Sole are brought in by the trawlers much of the year, and cod are ubiquitous on lines and in the nets all summer. In much smaller numbers ocean perch, tuna, skate, sturgeon and turbot are part of the annual catch. Shellfish such as clams and oysters find a ready market. However, as noted earlier, there is little demand for mussels, which exist in sizable quantities. There is a curious local view of mussels, regarding them as dirty and not fit for human consumption. (It might be observed that the Indians never had such idiotic ideas on the subject.) Crabs and shrimps are reasonably plentiful. There are no lobsters, although attempts have been made, thus far without great success, to introduce them to Pacific waters on a commercial scale. Crabs are caught in considerable numbers and are very profitable.

There is a modest attempt at 'aquaculture' with the cultivation and development of oyster beds at Sooke and in the Strait of Georgia. Unfortunately, water pollution has affected certain of the beds; for example, Ladysmith harbour was once a major area of production, but it has suffered somewhat in recent years. Such oysters as are raised are generally exported to the United States. Recently France has taken some of the oyster catch as well. It would appear that Canadians generally are less interested in shell-fish than other forms of sea-life.

It should be noted that sport fishermen account for many of the salmon caught in island waters. As an indication of the size of the catch, five so-called 'custom canneries' have been set up to preserve fish for sportsmen. In 1968 5,256 persons made use of these facilities. The charges made by the 'custom canneries' add to the general revenue.

There are also specialised curing concerns that operate on a commercial level. There are canneries for smoking all forms of fish, for pickling herring and for producing 'pseudo' caviar from roe. Both fish meal and fish oil are produced on the island.

Whaling, which was once a very thriving industry, has now ceased. As a result there are a number of abandoned whaling stations, particularly on the west and north coasts. Coal Harbour, the last station to remain open, finally shut down in 1968. In the latter years there were two whalers employing Japanese labour, but rising costs plus the shortage of whales were the reasons given for the termination of the local whaling.

The fishing industry brings about $12,000,000 (£4,800,000)

to the local economy. This is approximately the same amount as the cash income produced by various agricultural activities.

There is a small aquatic plant industry. A garden fertiliser has been developed which seems quite popular. As yet, there is really no great commercial use of kelp; however, in future years and with the development of new products, this is expected to change.

MINING

The mining industry has fluctuated from great activity to virtual passivity. Such is not an unusual situation in the industry, as any investor in mining stock anywhere in the world would confirm. In the early days the production of coal was a major part of the island's economy. Indeed, at its peak the coal industry employed something like 2,500 miners; this is no longer the case. Commercial production has now come to an end, for it is uneconomic. Gold and silver have been found in limited deposits and commercially mined at various times; they still are on a very minor scale, but they cannot be considered of major importance.

Far more significant are the sizable deposits of iron and copper. These are found in a number of places and the commercial exploitation of these deposits has met with considerable success. Iron mines operated until 1968 at Kennedy Lake and until 1969 at Zeballos; copper was mined at Jordan River until 1968. However, as these mines ceased operation new ones were in full production or in the process of development. Western Mines, on the south end of Buttle Lake, and Coast Copper, on Benson Lake, both produce a high grade copper ore. A new venture, Island Copper Company, on the Rupert Arm of Quatsino Sound has built an ore concentrator capable of refining 30,000 tons of ore daily. This mining company expects to be in full production by 1971, and the amount of copper and molybdenum will add very much to the value of minerals produced.

At present the labour force directly involved in mining is in the order of a thousand men and the value of ores produced is about $40,000,000 (£15,100,000). The chief market for the ore, particularly copper and iron, is Japan, and this country is likely to remain as the chief customer for some years to come.

Continued exploration for mineralogical deposits is actively promoted by private enterprise and the provincial government. Mining activity on all levels is moving more to the northern end of the island. In general, it would seem that mines closer to older areas of settlement are now worked out or are no longer economically viable.

The search for petroleum and natural gas has been very active. Various oil companies have been permitted to make exploratory drillings off the west coast. Some investigations as to potential oil sources have also been made in the Strait of Georgia. These activities have had very mixed reactions. The drilling on the west coast, on what is really the continental shelf, has resulted in a conflict of jurisdictions. Both the dominion and provincial governments have laid claim to regulate the activities of the companies involved in the search. The two governments would hope to share in the financial rewards if any be forthcoming.

The investigations in the Strait of Georgia have led to much opposition by various sections of the public. Reports of the disasters in the Santa Barbara harbour in California have raised the bogey of pollution, and with it the destruction of plant and animal life and the spoiling of many natural amenities, such as beaches and coastal areas generally. Ottawa and Victoria, in rare harmony, have proposed to halt all drilling activities in the waters between the island and the mainland, and the whole area is to become a national park.

There is a cement plant at Bamberton which was started in 1904 by Robert Butchart. He came to the island from Ontario and took over a lime quarry on Tod Inlet. Butchart's business prospered; in due course it was to be acquired by a larger consortium. The present cement industry on the island now produces about 5 million barrels of cement each year. Most of the cement is sold to local constructors, and with the increase in building it is likely that the cement industry will continue to grow.

FORESTRY AND FOREST PRODUCTS

Various aspects of forestry play a major economic role in island life. The island is still heavily forested and a very great number of the trees are in full maturity. Moreover, there is an organised project in hand and in operation to re-forest areas already logged over by earlier generations.

From the very beginning of settlement, sawmills were in operation on the island. In 1848 Douglas had established the first mill, while Captain Grant had one going in Sooke by the next year. Kenneth Mackenzie, who arrived in Esquimalt in January 1853, and who was to be bailiff of Craigflower Farm, soon had a sawmill worked by steam power at the head of the Gorge. He built Craigflower Manor and Craigflower School with boards sawn in his own mill.

Further to the north, Edward Stamp started his operation in Port Alberni in 1860. He had the third steam-powered mill on the island, and one which he brought out from England. After settling with Governor Douglas, he also had to make a deal with the Indians. He paid the latter £20 for 2,000 acres of land. It took him some time to get his mill fully working and it was not until May 1861 that the first boards were sawn. The timber was sold in Victoria and elsewhere. One of Stamp's memorable acts was to send a spar to England as a flagstaff. It measured 180ft in length, 24in at the butt and 11in at the top. It was too long for Captain Cyrus Sears of the *Pocohontas* to transport, so it was shortened by 6ft 9in. This flagstaff created a sensation when it finally reached its destination.

Stamp gave up as manager in 1862 and the mill was taken over by Gilbert Sproat. The latter expanded production, and something like 35 million board feet were cut in the next four years. However, such activity brought fatal results, for they ran out of trees. All of the trees at hand were gone, no more were readily available nearby, and transport was as yet too primitive to keep up the supply. As a result, the mill closed; the equipment was removed and the buildings abandoned. The final chapter of the story occurred somewhat later when the mill ruins were destroyed by a brushfire in 1879.

The story of another early sawmill is much more cheerful. Thomas Askew opened a mill in Chemainus—the Anglicised spelling of the Indian word 'Tsi minnis'—in 1862. This mill was operated by a waterwheel. Askew expanded his business by leasing some rather heavily forested land near Horseshoe Bay for seven years at an extremely low cost—it worked out at something like two cents per acre per annum. Like Stamp in Port Alberni, he sold his lumber in Victoria.

Askew continued to run the mill until his death in 1880, when his widow took charge for five more years. The mill was then sold, and was finally acquired by the Victoria Lumbering and Manufacturing Company. They modernised the whole operation; indeed, the first steam engine to work in a British Columbia forest was used by them at the turn of the century.

In the 1939–45 war the mill was taken over by H. R. Macmillan. It, thereby, became part of one of the largest forest products' complexes in Canada. The little sawmill founded by Edward Stamp in 1860 had developed into a major industrial enterprise.

Early logging operators were not really much concerned for the future. They cut the timber and then departed. Moreover, they were chiefly interested in the Douglas fir; other trees were regarded with disdain. Indeed, trees other than the fir were often cut down, treated as waste, and burned with the slashings. Large tracts of land were simply devastated by the loggers, and the countryside looked as if it had been the scene of an artillery duel.

Changes did come—in part from enthusiastic conservationists, in part from the government which responded to public pressure, and in part from the forest industry itself. The last now regards the forest in a very different light than did its predecessors. To the contemporary woodsman trees are crops to be harvested, but plans for the gathering of a future harvest must be made as well.

Forest land on Vancouver Island can be divided into four

64

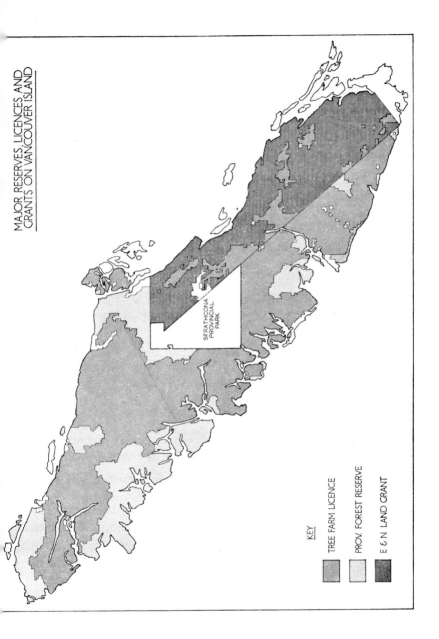

MAJOR RESERVES, LICENCES AND
GRANTS ON VANCOUVER ISLAND

STRATHCONA
PROVINCIAL
PARK

KEY

TREE FARM LICENCE

PROV. FOREST RESERVE

E & N LAND GRANT

65

categories. The first is provincially managed land—parts of the west coast, the northern tip, Kokish River area and the Sayward Forest. The second is provincial and national park areas—where, obviously, commercial logging will be very limited. The third is what is known as the Esquimalt and Nanaimo Railway Land Grant, which was part of the subsidy given to Robert Dunsmuir when he contracted to build the railway; these lands are privately owned and are concentrated on the east coastal strip south of 50°N latitude. The fourth and by far the largest area is under tree farm licences.

Modern logging now practises what is known as 'sustained yield', which simply means that the amount of timber removed equals the amount of annual growth. Lands available for logging are not sold, but are made available under tree farm licences. The government, which owns the land, lets it out on leasehold. On Vancouver Island there are 4·24 million areas of managed forest lands which will ultimately produce 18 million M cubic feet of mature timber. At present the annual cut on the island is over 300,000 M cubic feet.

The forest industry on the island operates as it does throughout British Columbia as a whole. Cutting rights are applied for by the company; the Forest Service, a branch of the provincial government, determines whether an area requested is available. In essence, the decision rests on the maturity of the growth. On the island, trees that measure a minimum of 13in in diameter at a height of 4ft 6in from the ground are available for cutting. If there are a sufficient number of such trees then a licence can be granted.

There is a definite plan in the process of cutting the trees; the most usual on the island is called 'block cutting'. This system allows for the felling of all trees, regardless of species, in an area of 1,000 acres or less. Trees are kept on boundaries or on the tops of hills to provide seeds and to act as windbreaks. 'Block cutting' is most satisfactory in areas where there is a heavy concentration of mature growth, and such is the situation on the island. In some areas an alternative system is used. This is called 'seed tree cutting'. All trees are cut except for a few isolated specimens in each area which are left to promote new growth by natural seeding.

Formerly trees were cut by hand, but now almost everything is done with mechanical equipment. One early practice is still followed : a wedge-shapel undercut called a 'snipe' is still made to determine the direction of fall. The tree is then sawn through at a height of 2ft or less from the ground. The fallen tree is stripped of its branches and cut into a suitable length for transport. Horses and steam donkey engines were used to haul logs until relatively recently, but now diesel engines have replaced them. The logs are taken to 'landings', they are then loaded on trucks which often carry 50 tons weight and taken to log dumps. Here the logs are sorted. In the past they were transported by fast-moving rivers, but this too has largely ceased.

After sorting, the logs are put into boom formation in a sheltered harbour. The booms are towed to the mills by tugs. They are kept in salt water for as short a time as possible, because they are liable to attacks from teredoes and other sea-life.

Periodically, as a result of faulty construction or inclement weather, a boom will break loose and the logs will come adrift. However, the logs are generally marked by their owners and can be recovered when they come ashore should it be thought economically feasible to do so. In 1968 special licences were issued to reclaim beached logs on the west coast of the island. Something in the order of 190,580cu ft were removed from the beaches.

Unclaimed logs are often cut up by private individuals for domestic use. Also on the west coast there are frequently great piles of bark which have come off the logs and drifted ashore. The bark is highly prized for burning in fire-places. Occasionally there are great piles of logs on the beaches which for various reasons have not been re-claimed by anyone. Local authorities then send in bull-dozers, pile up the logs and burn them. Fortunately, this does not happen often.

Very few people in the logging industry are actually involved in the felling of trees; only about 10·3 per cent of the total work force in fact. Another 25 per cent get the logs to the 'landings'; 14·6 per cent move the logs from the woods and make up the booms. The remaining 50 per cent are required to maintain the equipment, build roads, act as camp staff, work on surveys and conservation projects or be part of the large office personnel.

On the island there is a constant renewal of the forest since trees are harvestable crops like potatoes or grain. Silviculture is a highly developed science. An area may be replanted by natural means, ie, as a consequence of natural seeding, which is related to the plan of logging. Alternatively, and this is more efficient, seedling trees are planted by hand. The seedlings themselves are grown in nurseries—the cones containing the seeds are often collected by hand by young students and the like hired for the purpose. The small seedlings are put into the ground about 10ft apart and with reasonable growing conditions. This should produce about 400 trees per acre. As the young trees develop they are pruned and later thinned. After that they are allowed to grow to maturity and treated like natural forests.

One of the greatest hazards in the forest industry is fire. During particularly dry spells the woods are declared to be closed by the Forest Service, thereby minimising the dangers. A series of look-out stations have been built as observation posts to spot any conflagration that might occur. These look-out stations are frequently manned by students from the local university as summer jobs during their vacations. The Forest Service maintains a work force to fight fires, and now also uses aeroplanes which 'bomb' the fires with thousands of gallons of water. Fires may result from natural causes, such as lightning, or from human carelessness. A really terrible holocaust occurred in 1938 near Campbell River, when something like 70sq miles of land were burned over. All over the island are signs warning people to put out cigarettes and matches because of the danger of fire.

To emphasise the significance of logging on the island, perhaps the following summary from the provincial bureau of economics and statistics in their *Regional Index* for 1966 would be useful.

Vancouver Island has 6 per cent of the area of British Columbia.

Vancouver Island has 9 per cent of acreage of B.C. mature timber.

Vancouver Island has 14·5 per cent volume of B.C. mature timber.

In the year 1964 Vancouver Island had 26 per cent of all forest employment in British Columbia, 38 per cent of all logs cut in the province, 19 per cent of all lumber production, 58 per cent of all pulp capacity, 19 per cent of all paper capacity.

Today the island has about a hundred sawmills. These are situated principally at Chemainus, Sooke, Alberni, Tahsis, Victoria, Ladysmith, Cowichan Lake and Campbell River. The three largest logging companies operating on the island are Macmillan and Bloedel Company, BC Forest Products and Rayonier (Canada) Ltd.

Hand in hand with the logging industry is the making of pulp and paper. The first paper mill, on the Somass River near Alberni, was started by Herbert Carmichael and William Hewartson. It went into production in the early 1890s and made wrapping paper. It used rags rather than wood products, but the supply was limited and the costs excessive. The mill closed in 1896. A new start was made in 1918 at Port Alice. By this time the sulphite process had been greatly refined, and it now proved to be feasible to use forest products.

Expansion in the production of pulp was quite slow. Port Alice remained the only pulp mill on the island until 1945. Since that time, however, the industry has greatly expanded. Five large new mills have been built. They are at Crofton (pulp and newsprint), Harmac (pulp), Duncan Bay (pulp, newsprint and kraft paper), Alberni (pulp, newsprint and kraft paper) and Gold River (pulp). In the six mills on the island 3,780,000 tons of pulp and paper products are produced each year. This is about one half the entire amount produced in the province as a whole. Moreover, by concentrating on pulp products the local mills are able to utilise greater wood residues. This is because pulp has shorter, weaker fibres produced by the cooking processes as opposed to stronger fibres of ground wood required by paper mills.

In addition to lumber and pulp products, plywood continues to be made on the island and also its more modern counterpart chipboard. On a lesser scale, and more for local consumption, are pilings and fencing. The growing of Christmas trees for export is not a major industry, but is an added source of revenue to nurseries, farms and the like.

The number of individuals employed in the forest industry is reckoned to be more than 20,000. The value of their product is in the area of $525,000,000 (£210,000,000).

OTHER INDUSTRIES

A very sizable part of the population is involved in the tourist business. Indeed, so significant is the tourist considered to be by the business community that a full scale advertising programme is mounted each year. There is a semi-official agency, the Victoria and Island Publicity Bureau, which co-ordinates this annual campaign. The bureau receives money from many sources, both public and private.

The bureau has offices in many sections of the island. In addition to a programme of advertisement, it also gives away brochures, maps and similar material. Travellers write to the bureau or call at its many offices and it would appear to serve a useful function.

Visitors to the island generally seem inclined to stay only a few days, and all tourist enterprises are geared to this pattern. It should be noted that many of the visitors to the island, and especially in Victoria, spend quite lavishly during their sojourn. In fact, the amount of money spent is approximately twice that expended in all other regions of British Columbia. Moreover, this is not because the island is more expensive than other places.

Statistics indicate that about 10 per cent of all visitors to British Columbia initially come to the island. About one third of the visitors come from California, and studies indicate that they seem

Page 71 (above) The BC Ferry Authority makes communication with the mainland
an easy process. The MV Tsawwassen; (below) 'the Malahat', a famous section of
the road between Victoria and Nanaimo, if no longer an adventure in motoring
is still a scenic delight

Page 72 (above) Special dances are performed by the Indians. On occasion the white man is privileged to be an observer of these traditional events; (below) Thunderbird Park, near the Provincial Museum in Victoria, shows traditional Indian art forms including a reconstruction of a Kwakiutl planked house

to be from the more affluent part of American society. The average tourist spends a minimum of $20·00 (£8) per day during his stay. In 1968 there were 2,275,696 people, 692,231 automobiles, 8,115 American pleasure craft and 981 American private airplanes. The number of people and automobiles visiting the island increases by 30,000 each year.

There are vast numbers of facilities catering directly to tourists. On the island proper there are well over 350 hotels, motels and tourist cottages. They vary from the famous and elegant Empress Hotel in Victoria to a very simple cabin. The provincial government publishes an annual tourist directory which lists hostelries of all sorts and which gives such details as cost, number of rooms, and telephone number or address or both.

One major adjunct to tourism on the island are the numerous provincial parks—about thirty-five—varying in size from Petroglyph Park's 3 acres to Strathcona Park, with 530,319 acres. Many of these have excellent camping facilities provided by the government.

The number of persons concerned directly with the tourist industry is somewhat difficult to ascertain precisely. However, it will not be much less than 50,000 and could very well be rather more. Tourism in all of its manifestations is worth close to $100,000,000 (£40,000,000).

With the increase in the general population and with the steady rise in prosperity in recent years, the construction industry has inevitably profited. Many new urban developments have resulted. Construction of private housing has been very active; new shopping-plazas have become a feature of life on the island. The popularity of the high-rise multi-storied building for apartment living continues and these, naturally, have accounted for part of the profits accruing to the industry.

In recent years the provincial government has aided the construction of private housing with grants and other incentives. Set against this, however, is the steady rise of mortgage rate; 10 per cent is now normal and it is unlikely to get less. Second mortgages are even higher; 15 per cent is not unusual. In addition, interest

E

73

rate on mortgages is not deductable for tax purposes in Canada. Even so, building continues apace.

A very significant factor in the island's economy is the large number of civil servants who are employed by all three levels of government—Dominion, provincial and local. About the same number of people who work in the forest industry—that is, 20,000 —make up the complement of governmental employees. In addition, one must add the personnel in the Canadian Defence Forces stationed on the island. Both groups pour thousands of dollars into the local economy.

Vancouver Island has long been a favourite haven for retired persons with pensions, and clearly these pensioners are an asset to the economy. Every month cheques are cashed and the money spent locally. The retired and the pensioners increase every year. Consequently the amount of money added to the economy grows at a decided rate.

Shipbuilding was once quite important, but it is now very much in the doldrums. Formerly, Victoria, for example, had two major shipbuilding concerns, viz, Yarrows Ltd and Victoria Machinery Depot. Now, the latter's base of operations has been dismantled, while the former is part of the Burrard Shipbuilding Company in Vancouver and is very much the junior partner. Labour costs in western Canada are high and the necessity for the shipbuilding industry to bring *materiel* from elsewhere—the freight rates from eastern Canada are very heavy—combine to keep potential ship construction at a somewhat low level.

However, if few large ships are constructed on the island, there is a fairly flourishing small boat building trade. Since pleasure boating is so popular, the local shipwrights keep busy. Many of the trawlers and other fishing boats are built in little boatyards in the coastal communities. While this aspect of boat building may not be a major source of revenue, it is still not unimportant.

As is obvious in any society much concerned with tourism, there are many speciality and handicraft businesses. There are the usual carvers—the best of these are Indians—pottery makers and keepers of curio shops. Two local handicraft industries which perhaps stand out are The Island Weavers and the Cowichan Indian knitters. The Island Weavers were founded in 1932 by Mrs R. G. H. Murray in her own house. Attractive handwoven material—particularly woollen cloth for women's clothing—has a good market. The other island speciality is the justly famous 'Cowichan Indian Sweater' which is made by the Indians near Duncan and Kokisilah. These knitted garments are made from local raw wool in designs created by the Indians themselves. This small domestic industry was started late in the nineteenth century, the result of instruction given to the Indians by a woman of Scottish ancestry. The sweaters when completed weigh about 3lb and are generally in natural colours. They are much favoured by fishermen and other outdoorsmen, and have been presented to many distinguished individuals as examples of local handicrafts. In addition to sweaters, the Indians knit socks and tams of the same natural wool.

How is this economy in relation to the work force? Roughly speaking, a recent *Regional Index* published by the provincial bureau of economies gives the following breakdown: agriculture 2·3 per cent, logging 7·4 per cent, fishing 1·3 per cent, mining 0·8 per cent, manufacturing 16·2 per cent, construction 4·9 per cent, trade and service 64 per cent.

Generally speaking, the economy is stable and the inhabitants of the island can be considered prosperous. There are patches of poverty, to be sure, but the poverty is relative. There are constant efforts to bring new industrial enterprises to the island and it is obvious that the future will see many changes. However, it is equally certain that for some time forest products will provide the greatest cash income.

4 COMMUNICATIONS AND CONTACTS WITH THE OUTSIDE WORLD

T HE prehistoric nomadic peoples who visited Vancouver Island may perhaps be considered the initiators of sea communications. These primitive peoples were followed by the Indians, who moved from place to place in their canoes. The later contacts by peoples from the South Pacific and the Orient are further examples of relationships with the outside world.

With the landings at Nootka in the eighteenth century by Europeans, it may be said that more formal and regular connections were established. However, even these were still intermittent, and it was not really until the Hudson's Bay Company established its post that there was any degree of sea-going communications. The ships which came after 1842 brought a new way of life to the island. New settlements were created and with them came nineteenth-century civilisation. Each ship bringing settlers and cargo meant that Vancouver Island was less isolated from the rest of the world.

THE SHIPS AND THEIR ROUTES

The Hudson's Bay Company used its brigantine *Cadboro* for early trading activities. Indeed, the *Cadboro* was directly involved in promoting the early mining development on the island when it brought the first shipment of coal from Nanaimo to Victoria in September 1852. Other similar vessels were actively involved in coastal service. One of the most famous of these early vessels

76

was the paddle-wheeler, the *Beaver*, launched in England—
one of the spectators present on that occasion was King William
IV—and it took her 163 days to reach western North America
coming via Cape Horn. The *Beaver*, used largely to carry freight,
was a little over 100ft in length. She continued in service until
almost the end of the century; she was finally wrecked in Burrard
Inlet in 1893. The sight of the *Beaver* as it puffed along the
coast pulling into various little bays and harbours was one very
real indication of what was to come. The first steam boat to be
built in Victoria, the *Caledonia*, was laid down at Laing's Ways
in 1855.

Quite quickly a regular boat service developed between San
Francisco and Victoria. The service was greatly increased after
the discovery of gold in British Columbia in 1858. Would-be
miners and others desirous of reaching the goldfields took this
route. People resident in Europe or in eastern North America who
wished to seek their fortunes in British Columbia generally made
their way to New York, where they embarked for a port on the
eastern shore of the Isthmus of Panama. Here they were forced
to disembark—there was no canal until 1914—and take a train
for the forty-odd miles overland. Once on the western coast, they
again took a ship for the long voyage north to San Francisco.
Most travellers remained here for a few days prior to re-embark-
ing for Vancouver Island. The final stage of the expedition was
the crossing from the island to the mainland.

A good many men used this route, since overland travel was
not possible for some years. Consequently the port of Victoria
enjoyed a brisk activity for a few years.

Not all ships which came had the routine job of transporting
miners. Because men outnumbered women in the early days of
the colony, certain people in England decided to ship out a number of marriageable females, believing that married men were
more likely to settle permanently. The first shipload of women
never reached Victoria. Their ship docked in San Francisco and
they were quickly taken up by the unattached men there. The
Robert Lowe was more successful and reached Victoria on 10

January 1863. All the women who wanted a husband quickly found one. Indeed, for a long time any unmarried woman was liable to be plagued by suitors. Furthermore, few sensible families imported women servants unless married; otherwise they would lose them very quickly.

To illustrate how quickly local maritime service developed, in 1864 the mail steamer *Fideliter* made regular runs to Vesuvius Bay on Saltspring Island. Indeed, travel by boat was really the only satisfactory form of communication because the roads were generally inadequate. As a result, public money was willingly spent on wharves; for example, a government wharf was built at Maple Bay in 1875. There was now a weekly service between the latter place and the capital. However, not all communities were as fortunate; where no wharf was built the supply boats anchored off shore and cargo had to be transferred to tenders and rowed ashore. Early supply boats were the stern-wheelers— *Western Slope, Caribou Fly* and *Maude*—and the paddle wheeler, *Robert Dunsmuir*. All of the boats brought mail, freight and passengers.

Following the completion of the trans-continental rail line, the Canadian Pacific Railway began to expand its interests further westwards to the Orient. In 1887 it acquired three old Cunard liners—the *Abyssinia, Parthia* and *Batavia*—for service to the Far East. Two years later the Canadian Pacific acquired the imperial mail contract, which guaranteed the success of the endeavour. In 1891 the first of the 'Empress' boats went into commission. The three initial vessels were the *Empress of India*, the *Empress of Japan* and the *Empress of China*. Their distinctive feature was that they were painted white; the three original 'Empress' liners also had ornamental bowsprits with decorated figureheads —at least one of which still exists in Vancouver—and this added to their elegant appearance. Victoria was a port of call and many travellers to and from the Far East visited the island. In consequence, the latter was to become for many their retirement home.

The Canadian Pacific Navigation Company, with its vessels the *Princess Louise*, the *Maude*, the *Islander* and the *Danube*, began service to the west coast ports of Vancouver Island and between Vancouver and Victoria in the late 1880s. This company was bought out by the Canadian Pacific Railway in 1901. The latter organisation continued 'the west coast run' and now inaugurated 'the triangle run'—Vancouver-Victoria-Seattle. The new *Princess Victoria*, built for the purpose, made her first trips in 1903. Later other 'Princess' boats—the *Princess Sophia*, the *Princess Mary, Princess Marguerite* and the *Princess Kathleen*, as well as others—were put into service. All of the 'Princess' boats were built on the Clyde and they had Edwardian elegance; even those built after 1918 continued this tradition. The daily runs between Seattle and Victoria and between the latter and Vancouver took about five hours. There was also a night steamer service.

During the 1914–18 war the 'Empress' boats were requisitioned as auxiliary cruisers; the two 'Princess' boats, the *Princess Irene* and the *Princess Margaret*, were loaned to the Canadian government. Again in the 1939–45 war two of the 'Princess' boats, the *Princess Kathleen* and the *Princess Marguerite*, were taken over by the government for use principally as hospital ships. The *Princess Kathleen* was lost as a result of enemy action; the *Princess Marguerite* returned to local shipping service and now plys the Victoria to Seattle run in the summer.

The company was very fortunate throughout its operation in coastal shipping. It had only one major disaster—when the *Princess Sophia* went down on 25 October 1918 and 268 passengers and 75 crewmen were drowned. Inter-coastal navigation required a great skill on the part of the masters; there were many maritime hazards. It was said that the 'coastal ticket' for local shipping was harder to obtain than a 'deep-sea ticket'; moreover, it was also reported, whether correctly or not, that the company recognised the dangers and gave coastal skippers higher wages than they gave to the captains on the 'Empress' boats.

Today, the Canadian Pacific coastal service is virtually extinct. It still continues what is known as 'the Canadian Princess Cruise', which is a round trip between Victoria and Seattle, but even this is limited to the summer months only. The last remnant of the once famous coastal service is maintained by the *Princess of Vancouver*, which makes three round trips per day between Nanaimo and Vancouver. The *Princess of Vancouver* carries cars as well as passengers.

A couple of the old 'Princess' boats have ended their days as restaurants. One of them, the *Princess Mary*, is in Victoria. Old-timers who made trips on 'the *Mary*' are able to satisfy their nostalgia for 'the good old days' by having an occasional meal in the saloon.

Following the gradual withdrawal of the Canadian Pacific, other shipping companies—some of whom, to be sure, had operated earlier as well—took over the services. The fear expressed by residents of the outlying communities that they would be isolated proved to be groundless. The Northland Navigation Company of Vancouver has a regular weekly boat service for cargo and passengers. Their ports of call include most of the communities from Telegraph Cove to as far north as Bull Harbour on the eastern side of the island and from Port Renfrew north to Cape Scott on the west coast.

Another company, the Alberni Marine Transportation Ltd, has a service from Alberni to Ucluelet. Ships sail down the Alberni Inlet and out into Barkley Sound, calling at the various small communities along the way, and the complete trip takes a day. The company which operates this service has one boat, the MV *Lady Rose*, which was built in 1937 in Scotland, and as the advertising leaflet carefully indicates, she 'came out to British Columbia under her own power'. This is probably to allay any possible doubts as to her seaworthiness. The MV *Lady Rose* can carry up to a hundred passengers; her normal cargo includes mail and supplies for the inhabitants of the outlying areas.

Still another company operates a service in the Nootka Sound ports. The Nootka Sound Service Ltd has a year-round service between Gold River and Zeballos. The boat is named the MV *Uchuck III*. The regular run takes six hours, with calls at Tahsis and Esperanza on the way. Special calls are also made at the various logging camps en route; these are made by request only and are not scheduled.

Both the MV *Lady Rose* and the MV *Uchuck III* make special tourist excursions during the summer months. The *Lady Rose* makes a trip to Bamfield, while the *Uchuck III* goes to Friendly Cove. The latter excursion is of particular interest to historians, since it was here that Captain Cook landed in 1778. Both vessels have modest catering facilities but neither are luxury liners.

FERRY SERVICES

There is also an excellent ferry service run by the provincial government. Formerly all ferry connections between Vancouver Island, the Gulf Islands and the mainland were in the hands of private enterprise. This would probably have continued but for a strike in July 1958 which temporarily left the island virtually isolated except for air travel. Although the strike was ultimately settled, the government was determined that such a situation should not be allowed to recur.

The government first proposed to build roads and wharf facilities to improve the standards of service, particularly between Vancouver Island and the mainland. Various private corporations were asked to co-operate in the endeavour, but none accepted.

After further discussion the government decided to manage alone. In the spring of 1959 it set up a crown corporation called the British Columbia Ferry Authority under the general supervision of the Department of Highways. The latter proceeded to build new wharf facilities at Swartz Bay and Tsawwassen as landing points for Victoria and Vancouver respectively. Two new ferries were ordered, viz, the MV *Queen of Sidney* and the MV *Queen of Tsawwassen.* Two-hourly service over the 24 miles of water began in June 1960.

So successful were the new services that since that time more ferries have been added: the MV *Queen of Victoria*, the MV

Queen of Vancouver, the MV *Queen of Saanich* and the *MV Queen of Esquimalt*. These ferries all have excellent catering facilities, with both dining saloons and cafeterias. The trip from Swartz Bay to Tsawwassen takes one hour and forty minutes and the cost is reasonable: $5·00 (£2) per automobile and $2·00 (80p) per passenger. Over 100 cars and 1,000 passengers can travel at one time and there is no need for reservations. Only during the summer months or at peak holiday periods is there a chance of delay and at these times extra services are added. Mid-week travel is slightly less expensive than at other times. A special feature of the Victoria to Vancouver run is the 'Royal Victoria' Motor Coach—a bus service on alternate hours all day long and every day; from the bus terminal in one city to the bus terminal in the other in three and a quarter hours, and the complete cost for a round-trip ticket is $8·50 (£3·40).

In 1961 the BC Ferry Authority acquired the Gulf Islands Service. The MV *Mayne Queen* on an inter-island route departs from Swartz Bay, calling at North and South Pender Islands, Mayne Island, Galiano Island and Saturna Island. Many tourists take the entire circular cruise, which lasts about half a day and costs only $2·00 (80p). Saltspring Island has two connecting ferries: the MV *Saltspring Queen* from Swartz Bay to Fulford Harbour and the MV *Vesuvius Queen* from Crofton to Vesuvius Bay.

A month after acquiring the Gulf Islands Service the government bought up the Black Ball Ferries Ltd, which operated out of Nanaimo. Four ferries—the MV *Queen of Burnaby*, the MV *Queen of Tsawwassen* (taken off the run from Swartz Bay to the mainland), the MV *Queen of New Westminster* and the MV *Queen of Nanaimo*—sail between Departure Bay and Horseshoe Bay. There is another route to the mainland from Comox to Powell River. The MV *Comox Queen* connects the island with 'the sunshine coast' on the mainland. There are sailings approximately every two hours in summer and slightly less frequently in the winter.

In addition to these major ferry routes the BC Ferry Authority operate a number of smaller more local connections. Ferries run from Mill Bay to Brentwood Bay, from Chemainus to Thetis and Kuper Islands, from Nanaimo to Gabriola Island, from Campbell River to Quadra and Cortes Islands, and from Parksville to Lasqueti Island. Calls at Texada Island are made by the ferries which run between Comox and Powell River.

During the summer of 1969 the BC Ferry Authority, having acquired ownership of the Coast Ferries Ltd, assumed responsibility for yet another island route. The MV *Island Princess* connected Kelsey Bay with the northern communities of Beaver Cove, Alert Bay and Sointula.

A further link with the mainland is the entirely new service between Kelsey Bay and Prince Rupert which was started in the summer of 1966. The MV *Queen of Prince Rupert* carries ninety cars and 430 passengers. The trip takes twenty hours. The charge for car and driver is $60·00 (£24) but this does not include a stateroom—average cost $5·00 (£2)—and meals, which are extra. This is quite a long journey—about 330 miles—and may be compared with the ferries between Great Britain and Norway.

The BC Ferry Authority has demonstrated that it is possible to make the service financially successful. The service is reliable, the catering good and the ships spotlessly clean. It is a good example of the best form of government-administered public transport.

Two American ferry lines connect the state of Washington in the United States and Vancouver Island. The first is the Washington State Ferries; this line runs a daily trip between Sidney and Anacortes. The other company, the Black Ball Transport, Inc, links Victoria with Port Angeles, making two trips daily in winter and four in summer.

ENSURING SAFE PASSAGE

For many years a major navigational hazard of 'the Inside Passage' of the Strait of Georgia was Ripple Rock in Seymour Narrows. Ripple Rock was a twin-headed reef less than 10ft below the surface of the water. The passage could only be navigated at high tide, which meant that a ship often had to wait twelve hours before continuing her voyage, and these delays could be expensive. Unfortunately, Ripple Rock had been the cause of the deaths of 174 people and there had been over 150 wrecks—twenty of them major—since 1875.

Earlier denizens of Vancouver Island had hoped to utilise the rock as part of the foundation for a bridge across Seymour Narrows. This bridge was to bring the trans-continental railway on to the island. As an engineering feat it was theoretically possible but economically unsound and otherwise highly impractical.

Various plans were put forward as to how to get rid of Ripple Rock. There were a couple of attempts to blow off the top, but these failed, and, in the process, nine men lost their lives.

Finally, the engineers came up with an entirely original idea. A shaft of 570ft was drilled on Maud Island and continued from the bottom of the shaft some 2,000ft under land and sea to reach the central core of Ripple Rock. Two further shafts were sent up 300ft inside the twin peaks. Great quantities of explosives were then deposited inside the shafts in the rock. Finally, all was ready to set off the explosion.

During these preparations all the Mrs Grundys had been predicting disasters, with the result that many coastal communities expected the worst. The charge was set off on 5 April 1958 at 9.31 am. It was the largest non-atomic explosion ever contrived

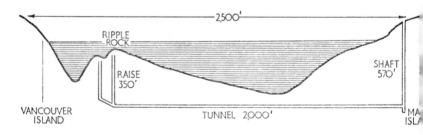

Diagram of the plan for the removal of Ripple Rock

by man : the quantity of explosive used would have filled thirty-four railway freight cars. The result was that Ripple Rock disappeared. A safe passage for ships was thus assured. Good technology had guaranteed success. Of course it was quite expensive : the cost has been reckoned at about $3,100,000 (£1,240,000).

Good harbours abound along both coasts of the island. Therefore, it is somewhat curious that the chief city had to have its deep water harbour created by man. Major ocean-going vessels simply could not use the inner harbour in Victoria. To rectify this situation, the 'outer wharf' was built in 1890. Two distinct wharves, one of 688ft and the other of 1,000ft in length, were built; this lessened the possibility of ships having to lie off-shore collecting and discharging cargo and passengers by tender. Twenty years later these wharves were further improved; a great breakwater of 2,750ft was constructed. This enclosed about 300 acres of water with depths from 35 to 80ft. In a further effort to make the capital a major port, the authorities built a grain elevator and a cold storage plant. There is a ferry-slip for the trans-shipment of railway freight cars. While a good many items pass to and from the island through this man-made development, Victoria can by no means be considered a major international harbour.

Ocean going vessels, particularly the freighters which carry pulp and paper products, are able to dock at Crofton, Harmac, Alberni and Port Alice. The new piers and sheds being constructed on the Rupert Arm of Quatsino Sound to enable the shipment of ore will provide major wharfage facilities in yet another northern community of the island.

To ensure safe passage for the many ships of all sizes the Dominion Department of Transport has established a number of navigational warnings. Vancouver Island has 22 manned lighthouses, 30 light buoys, 200 beacons and 200 other aids such as buoys and marked rocks. On Muchlat Inlet alone there are now 12 new lights which are needed as a direct consequence of the increased shipping tying up at Tahsis.

Although many of the lighthouses and buoys have existed for a long time, they have not been able to prevent all shipping from disasters. Many vessels were lost on the west coast in particular. Harlan Carey Brewster, who later became premier of the province, helped organise a rescue when he was a young man working as an accountant in a cannery. He was awarded the American Humane Society Medal for his efforts. The best account of the many wrecks and similar adventures is to be found in George S. W. Nicholson's *Vancouver Island's West Coast* (1962). In 1890, along the west coast from Victoria a telegraph line and parallel trail were constructed by the Dominion government. The telegraph was used to report any disaster and to summon possible assistance; the trail was used by survivors to make their way through the heavy forest. Along the trail were small cabins with emergency supplies. This famous 'Telegraph Trail' is now no longer in service and the whole has become somewhat overgrown. However, the 'Telegraph Trail' is very popular with hikers despite the hazards resulting from overgrowth and landslides.

AIR SERVICES

Air travel and transport is increasingly popular. As is the case in so many parts of the world, it has often replaced the ship. On Vancouver Island the aeroplane has opened up areas which hitherto were really remote, and vastly improved communications between many of the very small scattered settlements.

Faith in the aeroplane and its future was shown early. Only six years after the Wright brothers' memorable success at Kitty Hawk, 'a flying machine' was built on the island by William Gibson. It is said that Gibson's aeroplane was the first in the west. What is not entirely certain, though, is whether Gibson's machine ever got off the ground. There is some conflict of evidence on the point. A number of amateurs later built their own aeroplanes and by the end of the 1914–18 war flying was no longer a novelty. An early airport of sorts existed at the foot of Lansdowne Hill in Victoria and it was from here that one of the early airmail postal services was instituted. Mail was carried from Victoria to Seattle across the border. This pioneer attempt at mail delivery by air was not to be free from the usual disasters, which were more common in the early days of flying than they are now. It is reported that one aeroplane crashed into the waters of the Strait of Juan de Fuca and disappeared completely.

The first scheduled flights between Victoria and Vancouver started in 1933. They were not very heavily patronised, but had enough custom at least to keep them going. With the formal creation of airmail postal services in Canada, these aeroplanes became regular carriers.

The popularity of the aeroplane is, in fact, a post-war phenomenon. The Royal Canadian Air Force were the creators of the Patricia Bay Airport. Similarly, the Air Force had facilities elsewhere on the island, for example, at Long Beach on the west coast. These airports were to become landing fields for civilian aeroplanes.

Patricia Bay Airport now bears the additional name of 'International'. It is administered by the Dominion Department of Transport. A new terminal building has been completed in the last decade, and there are now plans to extend the runways so that jet aeroplanes can land. There are commercial landing areas at Long Beach, Port Hardy, Campbell River, Nanaimo and Alberni. These are all smaller than Patricia Bay and their facilities are much less extensive. Still, they are all more than adequate for the size of the aircraft using them regularly.

Air Canada has ten scheduled round-trip flights between Vancouver and Victoria. It takes about twenty minutes to travel from island to mainland. Formerly there were also Air Canada flights between Seattle and Victoria, but these have now been assumed by another airline. Trans-Canada flights, for example, terminate in Vancouver and it is necessary to change into a 'Viscount' to come over to the island. With longer runways it is hoped that at least some flights will carry right through. It is really only a minor inconvenience to have to change aeroplanes in Vancouver and it does preserve the island, for the moment at least, from the noise of commercial jet aircraft.

Other airline companies which operate regularly scheduled

87

flights are as follows: BC Airlines on the west coast and from there to the mainland; Pacific Western Airlines from Comox north to Campbell River; Port Hardy and beyond; and Island Air from Campbell River to the same general areas. Two airlines —Ocean Air Ltd, which operates out of Alberni and covers the Alberni Inlet, Barkley Sound and west coast generally; and Air West Airlines, flying between Victoria harbour and Vancouver harbour—use small seaplanes exclusively. These are particularly useful for charter and emergency services, since they do not require special landing areas and most of the more remote communities are totally lacking in air strips. It should be noted in passing that there is no scheduled air service from Victoria up island. One must go over to Vancouver first and then make one's way north.

The railway on the island manages to survive, but it is really only a shadow of its former self. In earlier days quite a number of passenger trains ran each day, but now there is only one, a little diesel-powered 'Dayliner'. A single ticket between Victoria and Courtenay, a distance of 140 miles, costs $7·00 (£2·60). Many of the old stations have been closed and replaced with regular flag stops. Special requests can still be made, however, for halts along the line. While the passenger service is virtually non-existent, the freight carried is considerable and this is what keeps the line in operation. The E & N, as the line is locally called, is a standard gauge railway.

There is also another railway which now carries only freight. It was intended that this line should extend up the west coast between Victoria and Alberni, but only a small portion of track was laid. This line runs from Victoria to Cowichan Lake and is part of the Canadian National Railway Company. From 1922 to 1932 there was limited passenger service which was then discontinued. Railway freight cases for both companies come from the mainland on special ferries.

Page 89 (above) The English rural influence is to be seen in the construction of much domestic architecture. This is a typical residence in Oak Bay but similar examples exist all over the island; *(below)* one of the few great houses on the island; Hatley Park, an Edwardian country mansion once the home of James Dunsmuir 'the coal baron' and now part of 'the Services College, Royal Roads'

Page 90 (above) One of the famous views in Victoria—the Provincial Parliament Buildings which were designed by F. M. Rattenbury; (below) Craigdarroch Castle in Victoria, built in the 1880s by Robert Dunsmuir, for a number of years housed Victoria College. It is now the home of the School of Music. Some of the rooms are open to the public

In this modern age a major road network provides the essential basis for inter-community communication. The automobile and the lorry are ubiquitous, and the miles of tar macadam road seem to be an essential element of contemporary civilisation. Vancouver Island is no different from the rest of the world in this respect.

Soon after Fort Victoria had been built, rough waggon roads to the newly settled near-by farming areas were found to be essential. Water travel was agreeable but not always convenient and often difficult for the moving of stock. In 1851 Governor Douglas gave orders for the building of a new road out to Sooke via Esquimalt and Metchosin. He estimated that the cost would be about £50. By 1861 the road had been extended to Cowichan. Perhaps to call it a road was being overly complimentary, for it was really only a dirt track of some 8ft in width, and was often virtually impassable.

The next decade saw only a slight improvement. A coastal road of sorts now existed between Nanaimo and Victoria and by 1886 a further extension was made to Parksville. In the same year there was a new road built between Nanaimo and Alberni. Earlier there had only been a trail. It took ten more years to build the coastal route to Qualicum—a distance of about 10 miles. It was not until the turn of the century that it reached Comox. By 1904 it got as far as Campbell River. Here it stopped until the 1939–45 war, when Campbell River and Kelsey Bay were finally connected. Now the entire coastal road to this latter point is paved.

The early roads were all unpaved: at the very best they were graded gravel, at their worst dirt tracks. To give some general indication of their state, it took about six hours to cover the 40 miles between Nanaimo and Parksville with a team and a buggy, and a day and a half by stage coach from Nanaimo to Alberni in the 1880s. Of course, with the advent of the Esquimalt and Nanaimo Railway, communications were improved but the roads were not.

A famous section of the road north up to the east coast of the

F

island is called 'the Malahat'. This was a re-routing of the old road from Mill Bay to Victoria. It was first surveyed by Major Macfarlane in an attempt to improve the rough track. 'The Malahat' was started in 1908 and completed in 1911. It is about 16 miles in length and goes over some rough terrain—at its highest point it is about 1,200ft above sea level. In the early days, 'going over the Malahat' in an automobile was quite an adventure, and the intrepid driver was thought to have performed a real feat.

The inhabitants of the communities situated on the western coast continued to travel by boat. There was a section of road constructed between the towns of Ucluelet and Tofino in 1912. This was, however, the exception and it remained virtually unrelated to the general network for many years.

Real progress on road construction is a feature of the post 1950s. With increased traffic, essential improvements had to be made. In the decade between 1952 and 1962 something like $25,000,000 (£10,000,000) were spent on general road construction and this excluded maintenance and the like. One of the most significant projects was the virtual reconstruction of the 35-mile section between Victoria and Duncan—this included the famous 'Malahat'. The cost for this alone was $7,900,000 (£3,160,000) or something like $225,000 (£90,000) per mile! The island does not have any American-style motorways similar to the M-1 in England.

More and more logging roads were opened to the public, initially on a limited basis, but gradually some were being transferred to the Department of Highways. While still somewhat rough in spots, which is to be expected on a gravel road, it is now possible to drive a car throughout the year on the west coast road between Jordan River and Port Renfrew. There is also a trans-insular roadway between Port Renfrew and Shawnigan Lake, which was formerly a logging road. In the near future, possibly, a logging road between Cowichan Lake and Port Renfrew may become public as well. Outside urban areas the speed limit is generally 50mph; within populated centres it is 25–30mph.

A major trans-insular road now exists between Alberni and the west coast. It connects with the road between Tofino and Ucluelet. Most of the new road is paved except for a short section of switchbacks, but this too will soon cease to be gravel. This new road has opened up a large area of the island for tourist travel.

At the northern end of the island it is now possible to drive on public roads from Beaver Cove to Port Hardy and to visit the west coast communities of Holberg and Coal Harbour. A road also goes part of the way to Winter Harbour. Port Alice, Rumble Beach and Jeune's Landing are now connected by road to Port Hardy and Port McNeill. There is also a good public road from Campbell River to Gold River. This is truly trans-insular, connecting two port towns on either side of the island.

Some of the logging roads are still completely restricted. Others are open on weekends and holidays. For example, one can drive from Gold River to Port McNeill through splendid wild and uncivilised country. This excellent logging road is about 125 miles in length. Of course, it must be closed to private traffic when logging activities are resumed, and the unwary traveller might have to wait a week before he can drive south again. There is a similarly restricted road between Alberni and Bamfield. All of these roads are two-lane and designed for automobile and lorry traffic. The traditional country lane, so beloved in Britain, really does not exist.

A quick glance at the map will soon show that even if one could go freely on all the roads, both public and private, many parts of the island are not traversible by any form of vehicular traffic. New roadways are constantly being surveyed; for example, it is expected that the eastern coastal road will be extended from Kelsey Bay to Beaver Cove in a few years. The distance is not great, but road construction on Vancouver Island is not cheap and the government must inevitably consider priorities, keeping in mind the whole of British Columbia. However, the island has only been settled for little more than a century, and the next hundred years will see many changes.

COMMUNICATIONS AND CONTACTS

One of the dividends that comes with good roads is improved bus service. Vancouver Island Coach Lines, for example, has three round trips daily to Campbell River, with more limited but regular runs to Gold River, Port Hardy and Kelsey Bay. There are buses also to the west coast on a regular basis. Areas closer to Victoria have a wide choice of runs each day. There are also some local jitney services between one town and the next. There are many taxis available to convey the traveller more directly and at his own time; these taxis are not really very expensive, even for longish journeys, if more than one or two passengers are included. For those who wish to drive themselves, but have failed to bring their own cars, there are the usual car-hire services. However, it should be noted that the number of cars available for hire is limited and reasonable notice may have to be given in some places to ensure that one can be delivered when required.

A visitor to North America once observed that everyone drove a car unless he was very old, very poor or very feeble minded. Vancouver Island is no exception. The bicycle as a mode of transport continues only for the young and the eccentric; the horse is only ridden for pleasure, and one never sees a horse-drawn vehicle except an occasional farm cart. The automobile is everywhere, and the network of paved roads both the cause and the consequence.

THE POSTAL AND TELEGRAPHIC SERVICE

Communications may be of quite another sort as well. With the coming of the Hudson's Bay Company and subsequent settlement, a need for a mail service naturally developed. For nearly two decades, however, the population was chiefly centred on Victoria, with only a small scattering elsewhere. It was not really until the late 1850s, with the increased population from the gold rush, that a more orderly arrangement became necessary. In 1860 a $2\frac{1}{2}$d pink stamp with Queen Victoria's head on it was issued for the colony of Vancouver Island. One stamp was apparently thought sufficient for the small population. Five years later a second series of a 5 cent (4d) rose and a 10 cent (8d) blue were issued. With the union of British Columbia and the island colony, the separate postage stamps of the latter were then discontinued. They are now considered to be relatively rare items and philatelists are always delighted to obtain them. A good copy of these stamps is worth about $50 (£20).

Each local community as it became established had a post office and a postmaster. The mail was generally sent up from Victoria by boat. As early as 1864, for example, there was a weekly mail service to Vesuvius Bay on Saltspring Island. Further north the service was bi-weekly. Various sorts of signals were made to indicate that there was mail aboard for the inhabitants before regular piers were built and ships could tie up instead of lying off-shore. The mail, with other supplies, was often brought in a dinghy to the beach. The story is told that when there was mail for Lasqueti Island in the last century a bonfire was lit on the beach at French Creek. The farmers then rowed the 10 miles to get their letters and papers. With the construction of the Esquimalt and Nanaimo Railway mail was carried by rail, but since the line was not extended to Courtenay until 1914 the mail boat continued to operate. Indeed, it was not until the aeroplane became common that many communities could get their post any other way. The Canadian Pacific boats were mail carriers until they discontinued service and their successors, such as the Northland Navigation Company and the Barkley Sound Transportation Company, still bring the mail to isolated areas.

After the mail was sorted at the rural post office it was usually collected by the recipients themselves. Rural delivery was a later development, and only when roads were constructed was it possible to carry the mail by horse and buggy to the various scattered farms.

With the advent of the automobile the horse-drawn mail carrier disappeared, but not until quite late in some places. The late Michael Bell-Irving used to tell the story that when he was farming on one of the islands in the 1920s as a young man the mail was carried by a man named Rob Scott who was a real 'character'. One day a tourist was sitting beside the road and he observed a buggy approaching at a high speed with a bearded figure driving the horses and standing rather than sitting. As the buggy came closer to him the driver shouted 'Stand up!'; the tourist initially did not comply and the command was repeated. By now the buggy was closer to him. Again the driver shouted 'Stand up!' and this time cracked his whip over the head of the tourist, indicating that next time he would actually strike him. The tourist jumped to his feet, the driver and horses went on their way without another word. Later the man asked at the local store what it had all meant. The reply given was as follows: 'Oh, that is Rob Scott and the King's mail. You see one does not sit in the presence of the King and Rob Scott believes that with the royal mail one is in the presence of the sovereign. That is why he drives standing up and expects that everyone whom he passes will do likewise.'

Private contractors took the mail on the rural routes. Individuals submitted tenders and the Dominion government decided which one to accept. During the long years of the depression a mail delivery contract was highly prized, and people put in as low bids as possible in an effort to obtain one as a means of having a cash income. Today rural mail is delivered by automobile; the pedestrian postman is found only in urban areas.

Letters, packets, parcels and the like are still not delivered to the door in the country. Rather, individuals have a mail box at the top of their drive on the main road. These mail boxes are generally metal with an opening in the front hinged at the top. The name of the owner is printed on the side. The mail is placed inside the box by the postman—in many areas the boxes are grouped together on the side of the road down which the postman drives, to prevent him having either to get out of his car or put it on the wrong side, so becoming a traffic hazard. Some of the boxes have a little signal arm which the postman puts up to indicate that he has left mail—also the owner may put up the signal himself to attract the postman's attention to collect letters as well—or the box may be completely turned in some way to indicate the same thing. The boxes are not locked, but there seems to be little theft of the contents. There is a more refined version of these local boxes. They are somewhat newer; they are always grouped together, often painted green, with the names of the owners on them; they are all kept locked—a symbol of changing times. The rural mailbox serves another function. Since rural houses have no street numbers and since many of them are well off the main road, and well down private driveways, the mailbox with its owner's name indicates that he lives nearby.

In rural areas that can be reached by car, there is a single delivery six days a week. In urban areas letters are likewise delivered once a day, but there is no delivery on Saturday or Sunday. Deliveries in remote communities are, of course, less frequent and dependent upon the arrival of the boat or the aeroplane.

Telegraphic communications were established when the first telegraph company was organised in 1880. The telegraph services were ultimately to become an adjunct of the two great national railway systems, the Canadian Pacific and the Canadian National. For a long time there were two competing corporations, but recently these have been merged into what is now known as the CNCP Telecommunications.

The trans-Pacific cable between Canada and New Zealand and Australia began operations in 1902. The line ran from Bamfield on the west coast and extended 7,830 miles. The Bamfield cable station was recently closed, and its operations centre moved to Alberni. The old station is now used for biological research by the three provincial universities.

The first telephone on the island was set up in Victoria only a year after Alexander Graham Bell had successfully performed his experiments. This early telephone in Victoria extended just two city blocks. A proper telephone company was formed in 1884 and over the years service was rapidly extended. The island telephone service is now part of the BC Telephone Company which is connected to the larger international Bell Telephone

System. The radio telephone was used extensively until the VHF was invented. The telephone is found in the vast majority of households on the island today.

RADIO, TELEVISION AND NEWSPAPERS

There are a number of radio stations on the island : Victoria has four, and Nanaimo, Duncan, Courtenay-Comox, Campbell River and Port Alberni, for example, each have one. Almost every community is able to receive some form of radio reception, since the Canadian Broadcasting Corporation not only has its local stations on the island but a system of relay stations also. Many American radio stations can be heard all over the island, in particular those located in Seattle and Port Angeles. Broadcasts from the Soviet Union and the Far East generally are readily received by owners with short wave radio sets.

Television is ubiquitous; everywhere one sees aerials sprouting from roof-tops. Not only are Canadian programmes received, but on much of the island American ones as well. The Canadian Broadcasting Company transmits programmes to the island from the mainland via relay. The CBC provides national coverage with a great variety of programmes. The CBC, like its counterpart in Great Britain, the BBC, is supported by the government and, hence, must serve all segments of the community. Individuals in charge of programming must cater for all tastes and for urban and rural society. On the whole, the public are generally satisfied with the CBC, but periodically it comes in for some severe criticism from very diverse elements indeed.

American television is quite popular. Recently the government in Ottawa has become more concerned about the Americanisation of Canadian culture and regulations have been laid down limiting American television. In addition the government has insisted that all television have increased Canadian content.

Although many pundits declared that the advent of television spelled the doom of the newspaper, such does not seem to have been the case on Vancouver Island. In Victoria there are two

98

daily papers: the *Colonist* and the *Times*. In the past the former was inclined to support the Conservatives and the latter the Liberals. Indeed, it was jokingly said that some provincial civil servants subscribed to both papers to ensure that their neighbours would believe that they were properly politically neutral. Now both papers are owned by the Victoria Press and are not particularly associated with any political party. The *Colonist*, the morning paper, and the *Times*, the evening paper, have separate staffs but a common printer. In addition to the two daily papers in the capital, the city of Nanaimo has a daily paper, the *Free Press*. While these daily papers do cover national and international affairs they also give considerable prominence to local matters.

Other communities have papers which are published on a weekly or bi-weekly basis (a couple appear regularly three times a week). These papers are very much concerned with life within the local area. The news of clubs, sports events, church matters, weddings and the like are given special emphasis. Among the numerous local papers published on the island are the following: *The Campbell River Courier, The Upper Islander, The Juan de Fuca News-Review, The Courtenay Comox District Free Press, The Cowichan Leader, The Ladysmith-Chemainus Chronicle, The Nanaimo Times, The Port Alberni Valley Times, The Tofino-Ucluelet Press, The Esquimalt Review, The Oak Bay Review* and *The Saanich Review*.

For anyone who wishes to understand contemporary life on Vancouver Island, and particularly in the smaller communities, a reading of the local papers is absolutely essential. The papers are the best sources of material for the historian and the sociologist. All the editors tend to be ardent advocates for the betterment of their communities and as such reflect the islanders' concern and interest in such matters.

5

THE PEOPLE AND THEIR CULTURAL TRADITIONS

IN any consideration of the people who live on the island one must differentiate between two very distinct traditions. The first is the culture of the white man—and for convenience this includes Orientals and East Indians, as well as Caucasians —and the second is that of the indigenous native population. To be sure, some of the patterns overlap or are contiguous, but many are not. In order to be rational one should discuss them quite separately.

POPULATION DISTRIBUTION

A decade after the first settlement at Fort Victoria, an initial estimation of the population was made. This semi-census disregarded the Indians and listed only white settlers. The total population was 450; of these 300 were in the Victoria-Sooke area, 125 at Nanaimo and 25 at Fort Rupert. Two years later the total white population had risen to 774, with Victoria having 232 residents. A chronological breakdown at this time showed that half the population were under twenty years of age; only fifteen were between fifty and sixty years old and *not one* of the entire group was over sixty.

By 1867 a new estimate was presented which included both white—this really meant all non-native—and Indians. It was assumed that there were between 5,000 and 7,000 whites, and about 18,000 Indians. Undoubtedly this was somewhat on the high side. The decennial census of 1881 included everyone; this

100

was the official enumeration of the people organised by the Dominion government. The published report stated that the island's population was 17,292. This indicated that the estimate of 1867 was, as suggested, overly optimistic. Since 1881, each succeeding census has shown that the population on the island has steadily increased.

```
1881 –  17,292
1891 –  35,744
1901 –  50,886
1911 –  81,241
1921 – 108,792
1931 – 120,933
1941 – 150,407
1951 – 215,003
1961 – 290,835
```

The next census will be taken in 1971, the centennial year of the union of British Columbia and Canada. It will very probably show that the population is close to 375,000. (In 1966 the government reported unofficially that there were 333,951 people resident on the island.)

The people are distributed in the following fashions :

	Victoria	Victoria-Central Region	Central Region-North
1854	300 (Sooke included)	125 (Nanaimo)	25 (Fort Rupert)
1901	26,514	20,513 (excluding Comox and Nanaimo)	3,493 (including Comox and Nanaimo)
1941	77,580	55,185 (excluding Comox and Nanaimo)	17,642 (including Comox and Nanaimo)
1966	147,312	167,096	19,543

The shift of the population is fascinating because Victoria for such a long period had a much larger number of people than any other area. The fact that the Central Region and the North now

101

have a commanding lead is undoubtedly a reflection of the increased economic emphasis on forest products and supporting industries, as well as mining and fishing on a much enlarged scale.

The ethnic origins of the population are varied, but not as mixed perhaps as would be the case on the mainland of British Columbia and elsewhere in Canada. Taking the total population as 290,835 in 1961, the ethnic breakdown is as follows :

British 204,169	70·2 per cent of the total
European 68,778	23·6 per cent of the total
	(4·4 per cent German and 5·1 per cent Scandinavian largest groupings)
Asiatic 6,523	2·2 per cent of the total
	(about 2,000 East Indians, remainder Chinese, very *few* Japanese)
Negro 103	
Indian 7,883	2·8 per cent of the total
Not stated 3,379	

(With such a small Negro population, for example, there is really no viable basis for a 'black power' movement.)

In 1854 it will be recollected that nearly 50 per cent of the white inhabitants were under twenty and *none* over sixty. The contemporary scene is a marked contrast to those early days.

1966—Total for Vancouver Island		Over 65	Approximate fraction
	333,951	38,289	1/10+
Victoria City	57,453	12,577	1/5+
Oak Bay	18,123	3,638	1/5
Nanaimo	15,188	1,717	1/9
Campbell River	7,825	358	1/22
Port Alice	1,383	10	1/138

The over-sixty-five age-group are decidedly concentrated on the southern tip of the island. The other regions have not attracted a large number of retired people. Moreover, conditions outside the Greater Victoria area seem to retain much of the frontier way of life and this definitely requires a mainly youthful society. However, in the next decade certainly, with the development of more

102

urban amenities in the north, an older generation will be less likely to move away to re-settle.

It is popularly reported that each year 1,000 new families arrive to settle on the island. Of these, about one-fifth are retired people. Most of them have previously visited the island on several occasions before becoming permanent residents. Interestingly enough, this increase of the population continues despite the fact that the cost of living on the island is reckoned to be about 2–3 per cent higher than the mainland.

BRITISH SETTLEMENT

Although 70 per cent of the local population is of British origin, a very high proportion are of Scottish descent. A quick perusal of any telephone directory on the island will show an inordinately long list of Scotia's sons and daughters.

Formerly a large proportion of the population was made up of a very special strata of British society. Oak Bay, Duncan and Maple Bay, for example, had a high proportion of retired naval and military officers and also colonial civil servants. These people perpetuated an 'English' way of life which, however, was not exactly the same as in England itself. Rather it tended to be a somewhat nostalgic and unreal re-creation.

Tea, cricket, the Church of England, tweed suits, and the like all were carefully preserved. At one time it was even said that there was a special form of 'Vancouver Island English' with its own accent which was used extensively by the younger generation. This accent was decidedly not English upper-class speech, but it was equally certainly not Canadian.

A section of the English community was presumed by observers to be 'remittance men', ie, they received a small allowance from their relations in Great Britain on the understanding that they would not come back. How many really did receive incomes with such provisos is questionable. Certainly a number had some private means, but a great many more did not. It is true, however, that there were often sudden windfalls of the odd £100 or so; everyone had the old aunt who died at a convenient moment.

The English community lived on Vancouver Island, but 'home' was Great Britain. It was amazing how well those in the colonies kept in touch with events; magazines such as *Country Life*, *The Field* and *Punch* and newspapers such as *The Times* were read avidly. It really did not seem to matter that they were weeks, even months, out of date. They provided the necessary contact with 'home'. In addition, settlers often had silver, pictures and furniture which belonged to the family and this was another tie with the Mother Country. Many of these colonial English never returned to the United Kingdom. However, they never really became part of Canada. They were in exile, voluntary exile perhaps, agreeable exile often, but it was nevertheless a very real exile.

The English community on the island were frequently accused of being more English than the English. Calling cards continued in use long after they had gone from similar circles in Great Britain. New arrivals were properly inspected before they were received socially. There was the usual colonial snobbery, but if a man were penniless but a gentleman, that was enough. He might work on the roads or as a logger—and many did—but he did not lose caste. An elderly Englishwoman put it precisely : 'It is all right to be poor in Canada but not at home.' There were eccentrics of all sorts; there were doggy and horsey people. These were laughed at by the ignorant, but they settled down quite happily for they had no doubts as to their own status. They were British subjects and that was sufficient.

Not all of the English fell into these peculiar categories. Many were good, solid, ordinary folk without pretensions. Some were of British stock from Eastern Canada; they were often more successful in their activities, for they had fewer illusions about life in a pioneer and frontier society. They were also more willing to accept local experience and expertise, not constantly preferring and comparing their earlier environment.

Today the various British strands are slowly becoming one. The two wars did much to create a feeling for Canada. The younger generation know only the island as 'home'. They are Vancouver Islanders, then British Columbians and finally Canadians, but they no longer feel British.

EUROPEAN SETTLEMENT

Other European immigrants made less of an impact upon the cultural patterns of the island. They copied the British-Canadian way of doing things. Few communities on the island were totally populated by people from the European continent proper. A number of Germans settled in Victoria prior to the 1914 war. There was a German club, for example, and a German beer garden, but these were to be casualties of the anti-Teutonic sentiment which arose in 1914. Emigrants from Sweden and Norway were found in the logging and fishing industries from early days. A number of Dutch settled after World War II, as did some Czechs and Hungarians.

One of the few areas totally settled by Europeans was Sointula on Malcolm Island. These settlers were of Finnish origin. Establishing themselves early in this century, the inhabitants proposed to set up a Utopian socialist community. The ordinary citizen of Vancouver Island somehow got the impression that Sointula was a free-love colony and, hence, very suspect indeed. This idea was quite untrue. Today the community no longer has its special social and political orientation, but few outsiders have settled in their midst.

NON-EUROPEAN SETTLEMENT

The number of Americans permanently resident on the island has fluctuated very considerably. In the colonial period they were quite numerous, and for a time there was a strong group favouring annexation to the United States. Many Americans have chosen to retire to Victoria over the years. They are generally indistinguishable from Canadians. In very recent times more Americans have come to the island, as they have also to other parts of

105

Canada. What real significance this influx will have is not yet clear. Moreover, whether they will remain permanently when and if politics in the United States change is an open question. While a number of people from all parts of Canada have come to live on the island relatively few have come from Quebec. There are no large French-Canadian settlements.

There was a small Negro community on the island from early days. Some were fugitives from the United States. The Negroes lived in Victoria, in Cumberland and on Saltspring Island. They were not always very well treated by the white population. For example, at one stage in the colonial period they were not allowed to join the local militia regiment, and had to form a corps of their own. However, the number of Negro residents has always been very minute, and they have not been subjected to any real discrimination. Their small numbers have generally ensured their full acceptance into local life. Similarly, the East Indian community is tiny—about one per cent of the whole population—and is fully integrated.

ORIENTAL SETTLEMENT

The Oriental community is a far more significant element in the population. The Chinese, in particular, have long been resident on the island. (This does not refer to the possible contacts between the Far East and the Indians long before the advent of the white man.) Chinese labour was imported to work in the mines and in the woods at an early stage in the colonial period. For example, in 1862, about 300 Chinese were reported working in the lumber mills at China Creek near Port Alberni. They also made up a sizable element in the total work force in the coal mines. At Union Bay and at Cumberland during the peak period of the coal industry, the numbers were reckoned to be in the thousands. The Chinese miners were generally regarded in an extremely hostile fashion by the white population, and there were occasional clashes of some violence. The white miners tended to see their Chinese counterparts as working for low wages under very bad conditions,

106

Page 107 (above) An aerial view of the City of Victoria. The Gulf Islands are in the background; (below) the Butchart Gardens, located in Saanich, have been visited by thousands of tourists from all over the world. In summer, concerts and theatrical performances are presented in this rustic setting

Page 108 (above) An aerial view of Nanaimo, the major urban community in the central part of the island. Nanaimo is a principal port and a ferry terminus; *(below)* beautiful beaches are a feature of much of the island's shoreline. Ocean bathing in summer is popular but the water can be chilly and not caring for anything beyond the collection of the money owed them. To a degree this was true, but too much was made of the matter.

The large Chinese settlements in mining towns have now virtually disappeared. There are still a few Chinese to be found in places like Union Bay, but they are insignificant. Most of the Chinese in such communities are elderly and they stick close together for companionship. In a way, they are the flotsam of life behind the tide of progress.

In the early days, many Chinese worked as domestic servants. In Victoria, in particular, they were extremely popular. In her delightful volume *The Book of Small* (Clarke Irwin & Co, Toronto), Emily Carr describes the typical houseboy :

> The Chinese all wore clothes cut from exactly the same pattern —long black pants, loose white shirts worn outside the pants, white socks and aprons, cloth shoes with soles an inch thick and no heels . . . They kept themselves entirely to themselves . . . learning our British colonial ways, keeping their own. When their work was done they put on black cloth coats made the same shape as their white shirts, let the pigtail which had been wound round their heads all day drop down their backs, and off they went to Chinatown to be completely Chinese till the next morning.

Many of these 'boys' came at the age of twelve or so and knew no English. They had to be taught the language and also how to perform the chores for which they were employed. Mrs Crickmay, an early settler on the mainland but whose experience was not unique, told the story that she generally hired these 'boys' at $5 (£2) per month and that she had to teach them everything. At one stage one of the 'boys' was moonlighting by cooking at a men's club and he earned more money than Mr Crickmay himself. The Chinese knew how to get on and how to save money.

In later years the sight of the Chinese domestic gave the 'old China hands' who had retired to Vancouver Island the illusion of the days of splendour 'out East' and implied a degree of service that no white servant was able to achieve. The Chinese 'boy' had taken on these functions because of the shortage of women

G

available for such duties in the early days and because the Indians were not particularly reliable nor very interested. Consequently, many households had Chinese cooks, houseboys and gardeners, and these remained a not uncommon sight until 1939. Since that time the numbers have dwindled rapidly. The Chinese also operated laundries, and peddled vegetables and fish from house to house. Later, many of them became the proprietors of truck gardens and small family grocery shops. They also worked in the fish canneries in large numbers. Their job was packing the fish into tins and later sealing the latter prior to the cooking. The Chinese were thought to be an essential element in the fish cannery until Harlan Carey Brewster introduced mechanical methods which made them redundant. This was thought to be a real revolution and his 'iron-Chink' for packing was hailed as a great and progressive invention because it meant that whites only would be employed.

For long periods the Chinese lived in almost ghetto-like conditions. There was a big 'Chinatown' in Victoria which had its own theatre, restaurants and other places of entertainment for the Chinese alone. The community was largely self-run and the various 'Tongs' or guilds kept things in order. Periodically, the Chinese meted out harsh justice to a malefactor from within the society. There was the occasional 'Tong War', but the white police rarely had cause to interfere.

The Chinese had their own benevolent organisation, established in 1884. A Chinese school still exists in Victoria; formerly the school had quite a number of pupils, but this is no longer the case. The young Chinese-Canadian is very much like his English counterpart, and wishes to emphasise that he is part of Canada.

The Chinese had their own burial grounds, as well, wherever they settled. The deceased were only temporarily interred. At an auspicious and convenient time the coffin was dug up and packed off home to China for final burial in the family plot. There are still many people on the island who can remember seeing Chinese funerals. The old temporary burial ground in Victoria, called

110

locally 'China Point', has now fallen into almost complete disuse.

The Chinese 'coolie' was brought to the island from Hong Kong. The conditions under which the Chinese travelled were very harsh, and not unlike those of the early transport of Negro slaves to America. Most of the workers were men and there was a good profit for those who organised the business.

Periodically there was considerable agitation to prohibit further Chinese immigration or to pass discriminatory legislation which would cause them to leave voluntarily. The so-called 'Oriental question' occupied a good deal of the time of the members of the provincial legislative assembly. In 1878 they attempted to regulate wages and hours specifically for Chinese workers and to institute a special tax of $10 (£4) per quarter. This legislation was declared *ultra vires* by the governor-general. Seven years later a head tax of $50 (£20) was to be paid by all new Chinese immigrants. The residents of the province of British Columbia declared this was too low; moreover, it did not seem to diminish in any noticeable fashion the number of Chinese who came to Canada. The head-tax was increased by the Dominion government in Ottawa during the Laurier administration to $100 (£40) and further increased in 1902 to $500 (£200). Uultimately, the whole question of Chinese immigration was to be dealt with in the normal manner through treaties between the governments concerned.

The anti-Oriental sentiment of the white community was peculiar. On the one hand, one element of the white population found Chinese labour extremely convenient and useful, but another group saw them as potential dangers to white supremacy and white civilisation. It must be remembered that probably some of this hostility was economic, but part was the result of propaganda about the 'Yellow Peril' and the Boxer Rebellion. Many islanders claimed the Chinese lowered the standards of public morality through gambling and crime generally. There are no statistics which confirm these views. More correct, perhaps, was the feeling that the Chinese were not real settlers. It was believed that all they were interested in was making money—ie, working

111

THE PEOPLE

for low wages with long hours under bad conditions—and then returning to China. Moreover, in the early days few Chinese had wives and families, and consequently seemed to be no more than birds of passage. The general lack of family life was not necessarily one of choice by the Chinese workmen, but one forced upon them by the system of semi-indentured labour. Ultimately, more women were admitted, with the result that normal domestic relations resulted.

In the last half century the Chinese have been increasingly integrated and accepted into the community as a whole. The younger generation often do not know the Chinese language, and are not particularly interested in learning it. The continuation of the ghetto tradition of 'Chinatown' is gone and 'Chinatown' is really only a curiosity, with a few businesses still catering for Oriental customers exclusively. There are occasions when the Chinese population do things as a community, but these are largely ceremonial or purely festive. The Chinese-Canadians are now lawyers, doctors, businessmen, professors, farmers and the like; they are no different from their white fellow citizens.

The Japanese were much later arrivals; it would appear that they first came about 1896. The numbers increased steadily, and soon they became as much the objects of concern as the Chinese. The question of Japanese immigrants was settled through direct negotiation with Tokyo early in this century, and these regulations remained in force until the 1939–45 war. The Japanese were largely involved in the fishing industry, and lived very much to themselves. They were not overly popular, and were regarded with some suspicion. Following the outbreak of hostilities between China and Japan in the early 1930s public sentiment became increasingly anti-Japanese. Nothing really untoward occurred, however, until war between Canada and Japan was declared in 1941. The Dominion government ordered all Japanese, whether Canadian born or not, to leave the coastal areas. Relatively few Japanese returned to the island even when they were permitted to do so by the government.

112

THE INDIAN

The aboriginal Indian must be considered separately; not only because the aboriginals form the third largest segment of the population, but also because they have a unique social and cultural tradition. The latter is not entirely that of the white man, but at the same time is not completely dissociated from it. The process of integration of the two traditions has been uneven and at times in conflict. The Indians now have wider choices as to their cultural patterns for the future. They can become an integral part of white society; they can live parallel to white society, enjoying its benefits and taking such elements as seem personally satisfactory; or they can live a life that is essentially within their own cultural heritage, largely apart from the contemporary North American world.

In any discussion of the original inhabitants of the island, it is necessary to define precisely 'What is an Indian?'. This would seem obvious enough—namely, an individual of Indian ancestry whose appearance supports his ethnic origin. But this is not the proper response at all. There are, in fact, two specific distinct definitions of Indians. The first is 'Indian by racial origin' and defines persons in this category with a racial origin in the paternal line as Indian. In fact, many of these people are not 'officially' Indians at all. The *legal* definition of an Indian is derived from one of the provisions of the Indian Act. 'Registered Indians' are those on a 'Band List' or 'General List'. These people are the only 'legal' Indians on the island or anywhere in Canada. One is recognised as being automatically eligible for registration if one's father be a 'registered' Indian. Illegitimate children of a 'registered' Indian woman are also generally considered Indian. If a non-Indian woman marries an Indian husband she acquires his status, and all children born of this union are Indian. The official status of Indian can be lost by 'enfranchisement'. An Indian may apply to give up his 'registered' Indian status, and become legally a white man. When this is granted the 'former Indian takes his share of the common property of the band or

113

tribe. His wife and family also acquire white status. None of them can return to live on the reservation, nor can they ever re-acquire Indian status unless a daughter marries a 'registered' Indian. Since all Indians now have the same political and social rights as everyone else in Canada, there is really very little advantage in becoming officially 'enfranchised'.

The coastal Indian has the same general physical features as his mainland counterpart. However, it should be understood that with the Indian as with the white man there are regional differences and they are as distinct from each other as are the English, Scots and Irish.

On the island live three general divisions: the Nootka, the Southern Kwakiutl and the Coast Salish. Within these general groupings are various linguistic subdivisions: North and South Nootka, Kwakiutl, Halkomelem, Comox and Straits Salish. Formerly Pentlatch was also spoken, but it is now a dead language. Linguistic subdivisions do not mean that all speakers are united in one common body. Rather, there are 'bands' or 'tribes' within the more general classifications. For simplicity one can refer to a 'band' as a smaller group, while a 'tribe' is the larger unit; the biggest group is the ethnic division. For example, one might refer to the Kelsemart band of the Clayoquot tribe of the Nootka. Even this, however, may be an over-simplification and some authorities might well have other ways of saying the same thing.

Early Trading Contacts

No understanding of the Indian population is possible without a survey, albeit a relatively brief one, of the history of the indigenous population since the late eighteenth century. Following the arrival of Cook at Nootka, Indian contact with the white man for many years was sporadic. English traders, 'King George's men', and their American rivals, 'Boston men', were chiefly interested in the fur trade. The sea-otter skin was highly prized, but so also were other pelts. The Americans were particularly active and were the more numerous of the traders. At the beginning of the nineteenth century relations between Indian and white slackened, although occasional visits by a few Yankee sea captains still continued.

The early trade with the white man did not seriously alter their way of life. The Indians gained items which generally improved their existence; even the acquisition of muskets did not automatically mean greater inter-tribal warfare. The chiefs became more powerful and were able to demonstrate their authority not only by force but also by 'the potlatch' or feast. On these occasions wealth was displayed and gifts were given generously; one's enemies were overwhelmed with one's affluence, since the receiving of gifts implied the giving of presents of even greater value.

Another of the developments of these contacts between the Indians and the whites was the creation of Chinook jargon. This was a trade language chiefly, with words from Indian languages, French and English. It had a limited vocabulary and was not difficult to learn. It was extremely convenient and became the *lingua franca* up and down the island as well as the mainland.

The early traders were treated most hospitably by the Indians in the main. Certainly, there was the occasional fracas, but on the whole relations remained good. The Indians received their 'trade goods' such as muskets, cloth, chisels, biscuits and trinkets which they needed and in exchange the white man got his precious furs. It was another form of the famous Atlantic triangle trade, ie, 'trade goods' were exchanged for furs which in turn were exchanged in China for silks, teas and spices which again were sold in European America; the cash obtained in these last markets was then used to finance even larger expeditions, etc.

The Indian for a short time really did very well. His own existence was made more agreeable by his acquisition of European-type possessions, but at the same time did not have the usual hazards following annexation and colonisation. One might well say that there was three-quarters of a century of positive benefit to all concerned. However, these semi-halcyon days were to come to a close when the Hudson's Bay Company established

115

Fort Victoria in 1843 and Fort Rupert in 1849. What followed was a sorry tale, but it did not all happen at once; indeed, as long as James Douglas was in authority, white-Indian relationships really did not deteriorate too quickly.

Governor James Douglas

James Douglas as governor and, as Chief Factor, really formulated Indian policy on the island, which was officially completely owned by the Hudson's Bay Company. The Indians did not own any land at all. Douglas interpreted this to mean that the Indians had no absolute ownership, but they did have certain proprietary rights. With this in mind, he proceeded to officially acquire land from the Indians in the name of the Hudson's Bay Company. For example, on 7 February 1852 he bought all of the southern section of Saanich near Victoria for £41 13s 4d—paid in 'trade goods'—and four days later he paid £67 14s 2d for the northern part of Saanich. He, thereby, acquired many acres of land for very nominal sums, though he did also buy the land even at deflated prices. Elsewhere, authority was not so generous. In all, while Douglas was chief executive of the colony he negotiated fourteen treaties with the Indians on the island.

Generally speaking, he allowed the Indians to retain about as much or as little land as they so wished. Since they were not farmers they did not ask for huge tracts and, as a result, everyone was relatively satisfied. It is true to say that in the light of the actions of his successors, Douglas's policy was most generous. Although the prices paid by the governor for Indian lands was never high, the little colony of Vancouver Island could not go on paying out money which it could ill afford. In addition, the imperial government would not advance any sums for the purpose, with the consequence that treaties in the Douglas tradition came to a halt. Those who came after him found his generosity not always to their liking, and the large reservation—such was the term used for strictly Indian land—was often re-defined on a less ample basis. Lands were frequently occupied without any form of compensation.

116

THE INDIAN

The Effects of Confederation

With Confederation the situation changed again—not always for the better—as events in the next decade were to show. Once the colony of British Columbia—and this included Vancouver Island—became a province, the Dominion authorities became responsible for the Indian. The transition was not easy. Moreover, most people in Canada really believed and hoped that the Indian as a separate cultural entity would vanish, and that he would become part of ordinary society. Old ways and traditions which were against the process of complete integration were to be swept away and all the agencies of the white society were brought into operation to bring this about. The church, the administration of justice, educational authority and the like fought against barbarianism as they saw it. They were remarkably successful, and it is quite astounding that as much indigenous culture remains as it does.

The Indian on the island was now administered by men in far-away Ottawa. There was very little that was personal. First they came under the office of the Secretary of State, then the Department of Indian Affairs, then the Department of Mines and Resources and most recently under the Department of Citizenship and Immigration. The civil servants were represented by a local commissioner. The first such appointee to serve on the island was I. W. Powell, who had his headquarters in Victoria. After 1881 there were three Indian agencies on the island—one at Duncan, the second at Alert Bay and the third at Port Alberni.

The main problem of the early days was resolving the question of land titles. Many people involved with the Indians believed that all of the problems would go away if the reservations were large enough and properly sited. Two Vancouver Island men—Gilbert Sproat, who had managed a lumber mill at Alberni in the 1860s, and then later Peter O'Reilly, who had been a gold commissioner—were responsible for the drawing up of the boundaries for the reservations. Nobody was satisfied with the situation, and it was not until 1927 that the question was supposedly settled. However, despite a financial payment, the whole

117

problem is still very much alive, and, as the Indians have become more vocal in demanding their rights, the whole matter still remains to be finally resolved.

Conditions Today

In recent years, most of the special restrictions on the Indians have been lifted. The Indians on the island, in conjunction with their contemporaries on the mainland, received the suffrage rights in provincial elections in 1949 and in the Dominion elections after 1960. Formerly no Indian could legally buy any form of alcoholic beverage, beer included, but by 1961 such limitations of civil rights were ended. In addition, the official disapprobation of old ceremonies such as potlatches and dancing was now no longer continued. The Indian could once again live his own life as an ordinary human being.

The Dominion authorities now have larger sums available for loans to make improvements on their homes, farms and fishing boats. In addition, the provincial government has established 'a First Citizens' Fund' which is to be spent exclusively on the Indian. More money is available for education and for vocational training.

All of this means that the Indian should get an increased share of the national prosperity. The Indian today is less willing to be the recipient of governmental charity. His income from money earned on the reservation is not taxable, but earnings from outside activities definitely are. As of 1971 there are quite a number of reasonably prosperous members of the Indian community.

The Indian agent still exists, but his function has changed; he is less a strong paternal figure and rather an adviser. The local band—a legal entity owning the land and having money—have an elected council and chief counsellor. The terms of office are strictly limited, but re-election is possible. Women have the right to vote and can be full members of the council. The band is the modern example of a communal society at work.

There are other changes. Education, which was formerly organised by various religious denominations, has now become increasingly secularised. The old 'Indian school' is being phased out and replaced more and more by integrated schools. This will probably mean that Indians will have much better education. Few Indians have yet entered the local university in Victoria, but optimists expect this to change radically in the next decade.

The health and social services given to all residents of the island are now available to the Indians. There are now no differentials in payments between white and Indian.

The area of employment open to Indians is theoretically unlimited. Actually, education and social attitudes do curtail employment possibilities. Fishing and logging take a larger share of the Indian work force; there are few farmers, but craft activities are becoming more profitable. For example, the Cowichan Indians knit thousands of woollen sweaters, tams and socks. One shop in Victoria sold about six thousand in a year which brought in over $120,000 (£48,000) to the knitters. Curios of all sorts are sold. Two local Indians, Mungo Martin and Henry Hunt, have brought the art of carving to a very distinguished level. Indians also work in canneries and do certain seasonal jobs such as berry-picking and the like.

Religion

By the turn of the century most of the Indians were Christians. The Roman Catholic church was active from a very early period. Father Jean Bolduc came with Douglas in 1843 and baptised a number of Indians. Further missions were established, one in 1859 at Cowichan and another in 1863 at Fort Rupert. In due course the Roman Catholics built a number of schools and churches for Indian use. The Church of England entered the mission field somewhat later. One of the great activities of the Anglicans was the Columbia Coast Mission, which not only performed a religious function but also provided medical services. Other churches had missions as well.

Almost all of the religious activities of the Indians are connected with the traditional church organisations. One only is distinctly Indian, and that is the Shaker church. This is a small

119

denomination which was founded in the late nineteenth century by John Slocum, a member of an Indian band living on Puget Sound. The church has Indian ritual, but it is Christian in belief. The 'shaking' is probably a form of religious hysteria but is regarded by the membership as a gift from God. The Shaker church actively practises faith healing. Shaker churches were built at Esquimalt, Saanich and Duncan.

Although the clergy opposed most of the old ways, a few aspects of traditional ceremonies survived. There are still 'spirit dances', which are religious in origin and take place in the winter and spring. There are also other special dances from the old days which are performed before an exclusively Indian audience; the white man is not welcome. At these special ceremonies frequently there are also speeches and songs in the Indian languages, which help to keep alive the earlier traditions.

One outward sign of change in Indian life over the past century has been in the acquisition of 'English' names. The early Indians took names rather at random; very often these were just English Christian names, eg, Dick, with the children called Johnny Dick, Tommy Dick, Mary Dick and the like. In the next generation the children of Johnny Dick could either be Jimmy Johnny or Jimmy Dick. (It is all a bit like the old Welsh system of Gwylym ap Daffyd, etc.) In some cases Indians translated their old clan names and the like, these becoming the surname. Others acquired Ango-Saxon surnames. All of this is symbolic of the final breakdown of the past culture.

Population Distribution

Prior to the foundation of Fort Victoria there were a good many more Indians living on Vancouver Island than today. Some areas of the west coast were infinitely more densely populated. For example, in 1835 it has been estimated that there were 7,500 Nootkas; this number fell to 3,500 in 1885 and to 1,605 in 1939. This pattern is repeated with the Coast Salish and the Southern Kwakuitl. The decline in the population was not the consequence of aggression on the part of the white settler. Indians on the island were not killed in active warfare. They died as a result of diseases such as measles, smallpox and tuberculosis.

The situation is now much changed. The number of Indians is increasing; the birth rate is about two and a half times that of the white population, while the death rate is only slightly higher. The population is very young in the main, too, which bodes well for the future. The following table represents all Indians in British Columbia, but the pattern is the same for Vancouver Island.

Median age 15–16	(Non-Indians 30 per cent)
35 per cent under 10	(Non-Indians 22 per cent)
23 per cent 10–20	(Non-Indians 15 per cent)
36 per cent 20–60	(Non-Indians 49 per cent)
6 per cent 60+	(Non-Indians 13 per cent)

Furthermore, 25 per cent are under 6 years of age; 50 per cent are under 16 years and 75 per cent are under 32! It is reported that death by accident is very high—much higher than with the rest of the population. Indians are, therefore, hospitalised more frequently, but they do not remain in hospitals any longer than the white man.

The number of Indians now resident on the island is estimated in a recent survey as follows:

Kwakuitl (including Alert Bay)	1,443	(North, East Coast to Campbell River)
Nootka	2,899	(West Coast)
Coast Salish	3,763	(East Coast, Comox-Victoria)

The largest concentration of Indians is in the lower Cowichan Valley and is reckoned to be 1,228. Indeed, this is the biggest single group anywhere in British Columbia. At Friendly Cove, where Captain Cook first met Chief Maquinna in 1778, there are now only 204 Indians. It is estimated that, assuming the present birthrate among the Indian population continues, by 1985 there will be one hundred per cent more Indians than there are now. This would mean that in approximately 1985 the Indian population will have been restored to the same numbers as in 1835.

121

THE PEOPLE

Future Developments

The inevitable question which faces the Indian community is what comes next. The Indian must decide whether he wishes to be fully integrated into white society or maintain his own individuality. It would appear from statements made by proponents of 'Red Power' that the Indian wants his own culture to survive and that he wishes to preserve his own identity. How far he can be successful in resisting the pressures to conformity is as yet uncertain. Increasingly, younger Indians are making their demands known to society at large. The Indian is no longer an apathetic entity who accepts the direction and the charity of the white. Various Indian organisations have been formed to speak for them as a whole. Such groups as the Native Brotherhood of British Columbia and the North American Indian Brotherhood have large membership and their lobbies have had more successes in recent years with the various branches of government.

Wilson Duff, in his *The Indian History of British Columbia*, Vol I, *The Impact of the White Man*, p 107, which was published a few years ago, probably gives the best summation of future development.

> The Indians will undoubtedly remain a distinct ethnic group for many generations to come, living for the most part in separate communities with somewhat different ways of life stemming from their distinct racial background, history and cultural heritage. There seems no reason why they should not attain equality in educational standards, occupations, and social life, and gain complete control over their own affairs. Their lives have changed drastically during the past century, and will have to change more, but they should always retain the right to find their own identity and develop their own lives within the framework of Canadian Society.

6   THE ISLAND'S SOCIAL
ENVIRONMENT

L IKE the rest of British Columbia of which it is a part, Vancouver Island has three levels of government—namely, local, provincial and federal. The local government presents a variety of forms, as it does in Great Britain. There are villages such as Tofino and Port McNeill, towns such as Sidney and Lady-smith, municipal districts such as Campbell River and North Cowichan, and cities such as Victoria and Duncan. All have forms of elected bodies with varying responsibilities. Naturally, the incorporated cities and the more heavily populated municipal districts assume a larger role in the social and economic life of the people. In most local elections party politics as such play no part, since candidates all stand as independents. All residents, if they be Canadian citizens or British subjects and over twenty-one years of age, are eligible to stand for office and to vote. However, only property owners may vote on referenda concerning financial matters.

Following the union of the colony of British Columbia and the Dominion of Canada in 1871, the erstwhile colony acquired the form of provincial government established by the *British North America Act* of 1867. In place of the governor appointed by London, there was now a lieutenant-governor named by the governor-general. The old colonial assembly was replaced with a provincial legislature.

Because of the vagaries of local politics in the early days, the

123

islanders elected a disproportionately large number of members to the provincial legislature. The residents of the mainland were naturally much displeased and, indeed, the controversy of 'island versus mainland' which existed at this time had this question of representation as one of its basic causes. By the turn of the present century, redistribution of seats in the legislature resulted in a more equitable representation. Today there are fifty-five members of the provincial legislature; of these, eight are chosen by the residents of Vancouver Island and the smaller neighbouring islands.

Since 1952, the provincial government has been headed by the Hon W. A. C. Bennett, the leader of the Social Credit Party. Of the eight members representing the residents of the island, seven are members of the Social Credit Party. Premier Bennett assumed office nineteen years ago with a minority in the house, but since then he and his party have increased their number of seats until now they have a very large majority indeed—nearly four-fifths of the provincial legislature are members of the Social Credit Party. Several members of the provincial cabinet represent island constituencies. The premier himself sits for a mainland riding, but even when the legislature is not in session he spends much of the year living in Victoria.

The legislature meets annually for a session of about three months. It is opened with all of the solemnity of parliament in Westminster or Ottawa. The speech from the throne is written by the government and delivered by the lieutenant-governor. Frequently, a state ball is given at Government House and on this occasion people from all over the province gather as guests of the lieutenant-governor. The present lieutenant-governor, the Hon John Nicholson, was formally a member of the federal cabinet.

The third level of government is the federal or national one. The islanders elect four members to parliament, which meets in Ottawa. At present, two are members of the Liberal Party and support the government of Prime Minister Pierre Trudeau; the other two island members belong to the New Democratic Party

124

Page 125 (above) The instant town is a feature of modern life. The community at Gold River was established to provide housing, shops, schools and other urban amenities for the workers in the Tahsis mill and allied industries; (below) not all communities have been modernized as this floating logging camp indicates. The floating logging camp can be towed by tugs to a new site when logging has been completed

Page 126 (above) The famous Long Beach over 10 miles in length—now a national park—with its Pacific breakers to attract 'surfers' from all over the world; (below) inter-island communication still depends on the small boat although improved ferry service has done much to ease the situation

—one of the several opposition parties in parliament in Ottawa —and one of them is the Hon T. C. Douglas, long-time leader of their party. The suffrage rights for the national elections are similar to those for the provincial elections, viz, age twenty-one, and either a Canadian citizen or a British subject. It should be noted that the Indians have equal political rights in all forms of local government.

In the past there was much rivalry between the island and the mainland; this was reflected not only in political but also in social and economic matters. In recent years this rivalry has largely vanished and neither party feel that they have any especially privileged position with the provincial or federal governments.

EDUCATION

In almost every instance British society overseas has felt the need to promote public education. It may well be that this is a consequence of the strong influence of the Scots in the colonial world, where education has very frequently copied the Scottish system. Vancouver Island was no exception to the rule and James Douglas, the second governor, was an active proponent of popular education.

Early Schooling

The governor had his own ideas on the teacher and the curriculum. He wished his teachers to be 'of strictly religious principles and unblemished character' and they were required to give 'a good English education and nothing more'. Douglas did not favour fancy subjects being taught to the young; he wanted the traditional three Rs.

The first school teacher on the island was the Reverend John Robert Staines. He was a Cambridge man from Trinity College. In addition to his pedagogical function he was to act as chaplain for the community. He arrived at Fort Victoria on 17 March 1849. He was given a farm and a salary of £540 of which £340 was for 'keeping school'.

The Fort School, as it was called, was soon in operation. In addition to the regular subjects, Staines introduced the boys to games—cricket and rounders, as well as boxing. Obviously, the British cult of sport was to spread to the colonies. Education was not free—parents paid moderate fees—but the company assumed the major expenses by giving the schoolmaster his salary. The girls at this stage were taught separately from the boys. When the Langfords settled at Colwood their daughter undertook to offer instruction to girls.

A school was built at Nanaimo in 1853, indicating that the authorities in Fort Victoria were convinced the settlement was permanent. In the following year another school was constructed for the children of the families employed by the Puget Sound Agricultural Company at Craigflower Farm. The bailiff, Kenneth Mackenzie, with five children of his own to educate, had been a strong advocate of the new school. The first examinations at the school were held in 1855—the occasion was almost holiday-like in spirit and concluded with a twenty-one gun salute. The original school building still survives and is the oldest such edifice west of the Great Lakes. Today it is operated as a museum, having some of the original fittings and also photographs of early pupils and teachers.

The first schoolmaster at the fort in Victoria soon became less acceptable to the authorities. Staines involved himself in local politics and became a vocal member of the anti-Douglas clique. The governor referred to him as 'a fomenter of mischief and . . . a preacher of sedition'. Staines was dismissed from his post; he left the island planning to sail to England, but he never reached his destination for he was drowned off Cape Flattery.

Edward Cridge, his much more successful successor, both as chaplain and teacher, arrived in 1855; his salary was about the same as that which had been given to Staines. Cridge soon became a staunch ally of Douglas and a power in the community. Both Cridge and his wife taught, and the latter ran a regular Sunday school as well.

In due course, Douglas appointed Cridge superintendent of

education. In 1861 the latter issued a report which was very realistic in its general appraisal of the state of education on the island : at Victoria, W. H. Burr was the teacher with 56 pupils, of whom 3 were girls; at Craigflower, H. Claypole was in charge with 23 pupils, of whom 8 were girls; while in Nanaimo, C. Bryant was the teacher with 32 students, of whom 10 were female. The schoolmasters were paid £150 per annum. The teachers taught all the usual subjects such as reading, writing and arithmetic; also there were some pupils learning grammar, history and drawing. Geometry only drew 2 pupils, Latin 1, but Scripture had 78. In his report Cridge noted, 'It cannot be expected that from twenty-five to fifty scholars are under the care of a single teacher without assistants or monitors, the schools should be in so efficient a state as might be desired.' He felt very strongly that there was an 'insufficient supply of teaching power'—a view which would be repeated by future heads of educational systems over the next century.

The Roman Catholic community had established two educational institutions for their co-religionists by 1860. For girls there was the Convent School where the Sisters of St Ann were the instructresses; this school continues in operation today. For boys there was St Louis College.

For those who did not wish to send their sons and daughters to 'the common school' there was the Collegiate School for boys —fees $8 (£3·10) per month for the senior pupils—and a ladies' college for girls—fees $10·00 (£4) per month for the older students. In both institutions there were some extras as well, for which additional fees were charged.

By 1865 the local legislative assembly approved the first *Free Schools Act*. There was to be a school board, a paid superintendent—salary $1,500 (£600)—and non-sectarian 'common schools'. The clergy could teach children of their own persuasion at a set time each week, but that was all. This was modern educational philosophy with a vengeance.

The results of this act were soon put into practice, with two divisions in each of the Boys' Central and Girls' Central Schools

129

in the city of Victoria. There were schools also in the Victoria District, Craigflower, Esquimalt, Lake, Cedar Hill, South Saanich, Nanaimo, Cowichan and on Saltspring Island. The cost for this ambitious educational policy was phenomenal—$25,000 (£6,000)—and by the summer of 1866 there were no available funds. Money was even lacking to pay the teachers' salaries. When the next school year began, however, the teachers, all save one, were back at their posts. They were not to get much financial remuneration for some time.

Following the union of Vancouver Island and British Columbia a new system of education went into operation. Schools were no longer free, the expenses were to be met by fees supplemented by the local rates. This system failed largely because local communities declined to levy a school tax; the feeling seemed to be that if a parent wished his child to be educated he could pay for it himself. Even the provincial capital had no free public education between 1870 and 1872.

Such a chaotic and scandalous situation could not long continue. Therefore, new legislation was passed in 1872 which created the system of state-supported education that exists today. Schools were to be established if there were at least fifteen children; teachers were to be certified; there was to be a board of education and a superintendent. Initially, this educational scheme was financed by the provincial government, but after 1888 both local and provincial governments were jointly responsible. Compulsory schooling followed in 1873, but this was for primary education only.

Secondary Education

Victoria set up the first high school on the island in 1876. The initial entrance examinations had 160 candidates from all over the island and some from the mainland as well. Of all those who sat the examination, only 68 were successful; of these, 49 were from Victoria proper, 14 from areas nearby and the remaining 5 from elsewhere. Not all who passed actually took their places; 8 failed to register when the school term began. Ten years later a second high school was set up in Nanaimo; its first class had 37 pupils. For a number of years following, students on the island who wished to receive secondary schooling had to go either to Nanaimo or Victoria. If they did not reside in these communities, arrangements had to be made for their board and lodging by their parents. By 1914 there were high schools in Cumberland, Duncan and Ladysmith. Thereafter, high schools were built in a number of communities, and today secondary schooling is readily available to most young people, wherever they reside. At present there are 14 school districts, with a total pupil enrolment of 92,673 in 1969–70. The schools are divided into the following categories : elementary, grades I–VII, junior secondary, grades VIII–X, senior secondary, grades XI–XII. There are still a few isolated areas without schools and these children can receive instruction by correspondence courses from the Department of Education.

For a long time the curriculum in the secondary schools was orientated towards the junior and senior matriculation examinations—particularly the former—which were given in June of each year. These examinations, administered by the board of education, were common to all schools. Papers were set in English (composition and literature), mathematics (algebra and geometry), French, Latin, geography, history and science (physics, chemistry and biology). The pass mark was 50 per cent and there was a system of 'supplementals' for those who failed, which could be written later in the year. Great rivalries developed between various school principals, each wanting as many successful candidates as possible. Moreover, every school wanted to have the student whose aggregate marks were the highest in the province. For many years Oak Bay High School and Victoria High School on the island and Lord Byng High School on the mainland vied for pride of place.

Gradually the school curriculum has become more general. There are now vocational courses as well as strictly academic ones. Secondary schools now 'recommend' on the basis of school examinations; as a result, a student does not have to write the

131

matriculation examinations to graduate from high school. However, students wishing scholarships for university admission must still take the governmental examinations. Senior matriculation —Grade XIII—is being discontinued in 1971.

Further Education

The provincial legislature formally established a provincial university in 1890. Provisions in the act called for the creation of a senate and a convocation was actually convened on 26 August 1890 with seventy certified members. However, the whole project collapsed following an acrimonious debate between denizens of the island and the mainland about the site of the university. It was not until a few years prior to World War I that the university was established, but then not on the island.

Following the failure to set up a university, the school board in Victoria made arrangements to affiliate the local high school with McGill University in Montreal. The arrangements were finalised in 1896 and the first two years of the arts programme of McGill University were made available on the island. Later, the first year of the science curriculum was added. Still later, the McGill University affiliation was terminated and replaced by a connection with the newly established University of British Columbia in Vancouver. Founded in 1903, Victoria College, as the new institution was to be called, ultimately moved out of the high school buildings to Craigdarroch Castle, the residence built by Robert Dunsmuir. After World War II Victoria College was moved to a new situation near the Provincial Normal School on the slopes of Lansdowne Hill. The Provincial Normal School —which had been established to train schoolteachers a number of years earlier—and Victoria College were to become the nuclei of the University of Victoria. For over a decade and a half after the end of World War II the college continued to send students from the island to the mainland to take their degrees. Following the report by Dr Macdonald on the need for university expansion, the first step was to make Victoria College into a four-year institution and let it give a degree within the framework of the

132

University of British Columbia. Then, eight years ago, the University of Victoria itself was created by the provincial government, with the passage of a new *Universities Act.*

Since it was felt that the site at Lansdowne was inadequate for any real expansion, land was acquired at Gordon Head. Part of the property was Hudson's Bay Company Endowment Land and part a former army encampment belonging to the Dominion government. This large tract allowed for a spacious campus to be planned. A number of lecture halls and laboratories were built; in addition, two residential colleges, named Craigdarroch and Lansdowne in honour of former sites, were constructed. There are three faculties : Arts and Science, Education and Fine Arts. At present, the university has an enrolment of about 5,000 students and grants the degrees of BA, BSc, MA, MSc, BFA, MFA and PhD. At long last the island had its own university and the argument of 1890 was finally resolved. The old acrimonious struggle of 'island versus mainland' became one of friendly co-operation between the new University of Victoria and the more senior University of British Columbia.

HRH Prince Philip received an honorary degree in 1969— the first honorary degree that His Royal Highness had accepted from a Canadian university. Other distinguished individuals— including Sir Edmund Hilary, of Everest fame, Christopher Tunnard, the eminent city planner and landscape architect, and the Hon W. A. C. Bennet, premier of British Columbia—have also been recognised by similar awards from the university.

The majority of the students enrolled in the university are residents of Vancouver Island and the Gulf Islands. There are some students from the mainland and from overseas, but they are distinctly in the minority. The University of Victoria, like Canadian universities generally, is not dissimilar to those in Scotland. Likewise, the student catchment area tends to be local.

A regional college bearing the name Malaspina College has also been recently established at Nanaimo. The initial classes were started in 1969. The regional college will ultimately offer the first years of the arts and sciences courses of the university, as well as containing a strong vocational side providing technical education to a more advanced level. It is likely that further regional colleges will be set up in due course elsewhere in the island.

Soon after the University of Victoria gave up its Lansdowne campus a new body, initially called the Institute for Adult Studies but now designated a regional college named Camosun College, was established on the old site. This new educational body was designed to cater for individuals who wished for further education but not necessarily leading to a university degree. Alternatively, it enabled students to reach matriculation standard who had failed to do so at some earlier stage. It has proved much more popular than had been imagined. There are both day and evening classes, thereby catering for a greater variety of student.

Private Education

Some independent private schools exist on the island, but their numbers are small and their enrolment modest. This may seem surprising, considering that the majority of the population were of English origin. However, in Canada generally the Scottish tradition of state-supported schools took root early and Vancouver Island was no exception, as seen by the *Free Schools Act* of 1865.

The private schools that have been founded are based on English models and emphasise games and character as well as scholarship. Their religious orientation is generally Anglican. Most of the private schools are no longer proprietary but have boards of governors and are non-profit organisations.

In Victoria proper there are several private preparatory schools for boys, eg, Glenlyon and St Michael's. For older boys there is University School, which was the subject of an article a few years ago in *The Illustrated London News*. Another school for older boys is Malvern House, which is now very closely associated with a girls' school, Westerham. Two other schools for girls in Victoria are St Margaret's—with newly constructed buildings on the outskirts of the city—and Norfolk House. St Margaret's School was founded in 1908, in the words of a local wit, 'to

134

prevent girls from being educated with Indians, Chinese and boys'!

For Roman Catholic parents desiring special religious schools for their children, there is St Ann's Academy run by the Sisters of St Ann, St Patrick's which is co-educational and St Andrew's School—formerly St Louis College but now only a preparatory school.

About 20 miles north of Victoria is Shawnigan Lake School; founded in 1913 by Christopher Lonsdale with six pupils, it now has about 200 boys. This school for boys aged thirteen to eighteen has gained considerable fame for its rowing, and on many occasions boys from Shawnigan have participated in international regattas including appearances at Henley. Not very far distant, on Mill Bay, is Brentwood College with a similar enrolment to Shawnigan Lake. This school was formerly located on the shore of Brentwood Bay, but following a fire, which destroyed the main buildings, the school was temporarily disbanded. It was re-founded about a decade later on a new site. Brentwood College and Shawnigan Lake are great rivals—insular versions of Eton and Harrow in this respect—with rugby and cricket matches being the outward manifestations of the sentiment.

A small school founded in 1935 called Qualicum College, on Qualicum Bay, has recently closed with the retirement of Mr R. Knight, the founder and headmaster. This was a small 'family school' and not comparable to Shawnigan Lake and Brentwood College with their two hundred or more boys. Qualicum College's enrolment was always well under a hundred pupils.

Prior to World War II there was also the Duncan Grammar School for boys, but this, too, has now vanished. Many years ago a very special institution existed near Duncan, called 'Skrimshire's' after the founder. This was really a sort of 'crammer's' in the old sense. It was very small and apparently specialised chiefly in coaching boys for the entrance examinations for the Royal Naval College at Dartmouth in England. At that time, a minute number of Canadians each year were admitted as cadets and 'Skrimshire's' had remarkable success in getting its boys

135

places. Skrimshire himself later joined the staff of Shawnigan Lake School.

Two private schools for girls are also located north of Victoria. One, Strathcona Lodge School on the shores of Shawnigan Lake, is not far distant from Brentwood College and Shawnigan Lake School. The other is Queen Margaret's School in Duncan. Both schools chiefly cater for boarding students, but Queen Margaret's also has a sizable number of day-girls as well.

The future of the independent educational body is much the same on Vancouver Island as elsewhere. Heavier costs have forced increased fees, but as yet there does not seem any immediate likelihood that these schools will disappear. Headmasters and headmistresses are aware that to obtain and to retain good staff proper salaries must be paid. In the past many young teachers were recruited from overseas—particularly Great Britain—but when they learned about the money that could be earned in the provincial educational system they frequently hastened to change their employment if they were able to acquire certification. As a result, staff changes were not infrequent, apart from the rare dedicated teacher, and both pupils and parents were not always happy. Now greater parity of salaries between the two systems exists, and, of course, there are hidden forms of compensation for the private school instructor such as 'free' board and lodging. Nevertheless, the next decade will probably see pressures for the continued survival of private education to increase rather than to decline.

RELIGION

With the exception of part of the East Indian and Chinese communities, the population of Vancouver Island is reckoned as 'Christian' in the modern usage of the word. The people cannot be considered excessively pious, but regular church attendance is, for many individuals, the accepted pattern of behaviour. Certainly in those areas in which a large number of the citizens are retired pensioners, the attendance rate is increased. In North

America it has been noted by sociologists that 'church' rather than 'religion' is the more significant; Vancouver Island is no exception to this pattern.

Probably the first Christian cleric seen on the island in the eighteenth century was part of the ship's company in one of the Spanish vessels. However, despite Spanish activity at Nootka, it would seem that little real attempt was made at converting the Indians—although Padre Catala is portrayed in a window at St Pius X Church on Nootka Island in the act of preaching to the native peoples. Considering the Spanish historical tradition, it is somewhat surprising that much more was not done. What would have occurred had the Spanish settlement at Nootka continued is an open question, but it is reasonable to assume that a mission or series of missions would have been built, as in other Spanish colonies in the North and South American continents.

It was not until James Douglas arrived in 1843 to set up the Hudson's Bay fort that any major attempt at Christian proselytising was begun. Accompanying the Chief Factor was Father Jean-Baptiste Bolduc, who baptised a number of the local Songhee band (part of the Coast Salish tribe). He was followed in his activities by Father Lamfrit, who served on the island from 1849 to 1852 and who is reckoned to have baptised over 3,000 natives. Other religious denominations soon followed.

The Catholic Church

The Roman Catholics were quick to extend their activities throughout the island. A series of churches were built to accommodate the Indians and the new settlers. A list of churches built in the nineteenth century gives a clearer indication of what was accomplished in short order.

St Joseph's	Esquimalt	1849
St Andrew's	Victoria	1858
St Ann's	Cowichan	1858
St Peter's	Nanaimo	1864
St Louis	Victoria	1864
Assumption	Saanich	1869
Sacred Heart	Hesquiot	1875

137

Purification	Comox	1878
St Leo	Numkus	1879
St John the Baptist	Kyuquot	1880
Holy Rosary	Penalgut	1881
St Andrew's (new building and cathedral)	Victoria	1892

The Roman Catholic communion now has churches in almost every community and settlement. For example, recent construction has seen the following new buildings:

Ucluelet	Holy Family	1953
Tofino	St Francis of Assisi	1963
Port Hardy	St Bonadventure	1969

Many new churches have been built to meet the needs of the growing urban population. The Roman Catholics have utilised the talents of various local architects—notably in recent years John Di Castri—and have built some fine and interesting buildings. Indeed, they have perhaps been more architecturally experimental than other religious bodies.

Very early in the missionary work of the Roman Catholics it was seen that a female religious order was necessary. The Sisters of St Ann established a convent, a school and a hospital in Victoria. Later they opened convents at Cowichan and Nanaimo.

The first Roman Catholic bishop was Modeste Demers, who arrived on 29 August 1852. He came by canoe and was accompanied by Father Lootems, who was later to become the first Bishop of Idaho in the United States. The bishopric of Vancouver Island was extremely extensive and included the mainland of British Columbia and Alaska. It was subdivided in 1863; Bishop Demers retained Vancouver Island and Alaska until his death in 1871. His successor, Charles Seghers, was appointed in 1873, remaining in the see until 1879 when he became Archbishop of Portland. Retiring in 1885, he returned at his own request to Vancouver Island. He did not long enjoy his position, for he was assassinated on a visit to Alaska in 1886.

In due course, Alaska and the island were organised as separate dioceses. The island see bears the name of the bishopric of Victoria. The present incumbent is Bishop Remi de Roo. Currently there are 33,000 members of the church in the diocese.

The Anglican Church

If the Roman Catholics were the first on the ground, their Anglican brethren, arriving only a short time later, initially had the better position. Indeed, one might also say that the Church of England was an endowed institution. The company appointed a chaplain for their post, paid his salary and gave him a glebe farm.

The first chaplain, Robert John Staines, arrived with his wife on 17 March 1849. As there was not yet any church building, he conducted the Sunday services in the fort itself. In order to rectify this state of affairs, the cornerstone of the first church was laid in 1853 and completed in 1856.

After Staines left the island, Edward Cridge arrived in 1855. Cridge was to become one of the great characters of colonial society. With the ending of the Hudson's Bay Company's monopolistic status by the Crown, some changes were made in the religious establishment. The Colonial Office did not intend that any church be formally 'established'. All religious bodies were on equal terms.

With the formal establishment of an episcopal see, the story of Douglas and Blanshard was repeated all over again, ie, Cridge, the man on the spot, was not named to the episcopate, as would have been both sensible and extremely popular. Instead, George Hills was appointed in 1858. The fledgling see received a donation of £25,000 from the Baroness Burdett-Coutts as a form of endowment. Bishop Hills arrived in January 1860.

There were now two Anglican churches in Victoria—Christ Church, which became the cathedral with Edward Cridge as dean, and St John's, 'the iron church', which was the newer edifice. The latter had cost $13,000 (£5,200) and seated 650. The original Christ Church building was destroyed by fire a little more than a decade later, but was rapidly rebuilt.

Christian harmony did not long prevail in Anglican circles. A dreadful quarrel broke out between Hills and Cridge. The

139

former was generally tractarian in outlook, while the latter was latitudinarian. After an ecclesiastical trial and a civil suit, a schism occurred in 1874. Cridge and his supporters established the Reformed Episcopal Church—land for the church building was given by Sir James Douglas, who joined the newly created denomination, and a few years later his funeral services were conducted by Cridge from this church. The original wooden building still stands and is still used for regular services.

Edward Cridge himself was made a bishop in Chicago in 1875 by the Episcopal Church and consecrated a year later. He lived to a great age and was a very prominent figure until his death. There was no rapprochement of any sort between the Anglicans and the Reformed Episcopalians for many years. However, when the original protagonists and their supporters died, the situation was to change. While the Reformed Episcopal Church continues to be separate from the Church of England in Canada the two communions are very friendly, and the old hostility between them no longer exists.

Although the official Anglican communion was somewhat diminished by the secession of Hill's opponents, the church itself continued to develop. It became increasingly clear that the old diocesan arrangements would have to change. In 1879 the see was divided into three—New Westminster, Caledonia and Columbia. Vancouver Island was in the last named and Christ Church Cathedral in Victoria was the episcopal headquarters.

As settlement had extended beyond Fort Victoria, more churches were constructed by the Anglicans to serve the new communities. Nanaimo established its own church, St Paul's, in 1862. In this same year St Stephen's was erected in Saanich. In part, this church is built with redwood imported from California, since there was no sawmill in the area to cut the necessary lumber. Other early churches were All Saints' at Westholme and St Peter's at Quamichan. The latter is of considerable interest historically, as its old churchyard contains the graves of many of the early residents of the Cowichan area. Moreover, the war memorial in this same churchyard shows very poignantly why the Cowichan

140

area of post-1918 was never quite the same again. St Anne's Church near Parksville is entirely constructed of logs. Established in 1894, largely through the efforts of the Reverend C. E. Cooper, it was built almost entirely by voluntary labour. The Anglicans also had a naval and garrison church, St Paul's, in Esquimalt. All of these churches are still in regular use.

Almost every community on the island now has an Anglican church. (Properly speaking, one should refer to the communion as the Church of England in Canada, but popularly the name Anglican is always used.) For many years the more remote communities were served by the Columbia Coast Mission, which made regular visits.

Columbia Coast Mission

This organisation was founded in 1905 as a consequence of the Reverend John Antle's journey up the west coast of the island the year previously. Antle's intention on his trip was to write a report on the medical facilities available to the remote communities and the logging camps. As a result of his tour he found there was an acute shortage of such services and the need was dire, since the nearest hospitals were often 200 miles away. Antle—'the Grenfell of the West'—was aware that the religious side must play a secondary role to social and medical needs. When the men were on 'your side' you could then preach and hope to bring them to the church.

The first boat, the *Columbia I*, was launched in 1905 and replaced by *Columbia II* five years later. The latter boat was much larger than the first and had considerable hospital facilities aboard. It made regular calls—ninety-two at one time—at various ports and also was available in emergencies. The *Columbia II*, until it was sold in 1955, was the principal vessel operated by the mission. There were other ships—about a dozen in all—in use at various times. The main rendezvous for all the boats was at Quathiaski Cove on Quadra Island. The Reverend Alan Greene was in charge here during the 1920's and 1930's and he succeeded Antle as general superintendent in 1936.

In addition to the boats, the mission had hospitals at Rock Bay, Alert Bay, Pender Harbour (on the mainland) and Village Island (a tuberculosis sanatorium). For a brief time there was a hospital at Vananda on Texada Island. In the 1920s there was also a regular floating hospital, but this was wrecked in 1928 while being towed from one logging camp to another. The Rock Bay Hospital was important because of the logging activities, but when these declined the buildings were sold and became a fishing lodge.

The Columbia Coast Mission also built churches and organised regular parishes. Thus, religion and social service went hand in hand. Antle and Green were joined by a number of clergy over the years who often served for many years.

The mission's history can be summarised quickly: 1905–12, a period of great activity and expansion; 1914–18, acute staffing problems because of the war; 1920–30, a time of regularity and order; 1930–39, much activity and mission relief—often the only form of aid during the depression; 1939–45, again staffing problems and use consequently of older men; 1950–60, superficially a bright period with new boats built and considerable recognition in the golden jubilee year of 1955; 1960–70, rapid decline as the need for such service dwindled with improved communications and more settled communities. Aeroplanes were more available and provided better service—the United Church, for example, had used them for quite a long time.

The mission no longer operates as it did in the past. The regular parochial work is now done through the diocese of Columbia. The mission ships are part of history. Antle and his successor Greene will go down as real pioneers, and receive their just plaudits from posterity.

Modern Developments

A figure of considerable significance for a long time in the local Anglican diocese was Harold Sexton, who served as bishop from the middle 1930s until his recent retirement. For a period he was also archbishop when he became the primate of Western Canada.

142

Page 143 *(above left)* The plaque commemorating the discovery of Nootka Sound by Captain Cook; *(above right)* Sir James Douglas, the second governor of the colony of Vancouver Island and the true founder of the settlement; *(below left)* early settlers built a number of churches. Although modelled on the traditional English style, they were constructed of wood rather than of brick and stone; *(below right)* 'The Bastion', a central feature of the fort built by Sir James Douglas at Nanaimo. The fort itself has long disappeared, only 'The Bastion' remains and it has been re-sited. It is now a museum

Page 144 (above left) Mungo Martin and his son, among the few professional carvers, are two of the great artists still making totem poles. Most carving is done by amateurs; (above right) 'Cowichan Indian Sweaters' knitted by native women is a thriving domestic industry. The hand-spun and hand-knitted natural wool makes splendid sweaters with traditional designs; (below left) Elk Falls near Campbell River. The island abounds in many waterfalls but few are so spectacular; (below right) steelhead are a form of rainbow trout that migrate to the sea. Many local anglers consider steelhead fishing the best piscatorial sport on the Pacific Coast. The fish are caught with a fly or spinner in the late autumn and in the winter

Archbishop Sexton was a much beloved public figure and a champion of many liberal causes.

There are several examples of the contemporary ecumenical movement and church co-operation between Roman Catholics and Anglicans. The two religious organisations share churches at Gold River, Rumble Beach and Port McNeill. At Port Alice and Porty Hardy, the Anglicans share church buildings with the United Church of Canada.

Today there are approximately 28,500 practising Anglicans on Vancouver Island and a further 1,900 on the neighbouring Gulf Islands. Probably there are a good many other nominal members of the church, but these have not been officially recognised as such. The present cathedral church building was begun in 1929 during the episcopate of Bishop Schofield. It is in the classical tradition of church architecture, being English Gothic in design. During the depression years work continued, but progress was very slow. The original plans have been much altered, and the rather grandiose ambitions somewhat curtailed. The building as it now stands, with its two great west towers, is really only the nave of what might have been a huge structure. The plans for a spire seem to have been abandoned, and further enlargement, such as adding the usual crossing and the choir, now seems unlikely in the near future. The present building is quite adequate for ordinary church purposes. Internally, it is very plain, with few decorative features. One charming conceit is a carved stone robin and nest. This was the work of one of the artisans, who had observed in an early stage of building that a live robin had actually nested inside the incomplete edifice. Few, if any, really feel that Christ Church Cathedral needs any further additions, and while this is perhaps artistically unsatisfactory, it is certainly a recognition of present reality.

Other Denominations

The Methodists arrived in 1858 and built their first church in 1859. With a nice ecumenical spirit, Governor Douglas, an Anglican, laid the cornerstone. The land for this church was given by the Hudson's Bay Company. The Methodists built a church in Nanaimo in 1860. They had special missions to the Chinese and the Indians. Two of the most fascinating accounts of early mission work are by Thomas Crosby, who arrived in 1862 and worked for seven years with the Indians. These volumes, *Among the Ankomenums* (1907) and *Up and Down the North Pacific Coast by Canoe and Mission Ship* (1914), tell of his experiences in a most splendid fashion. With the formation of the BC Methodist Conference in 1887 the island churches joined it. The Methodists continued to be active in church expansion, with Sunday schools as a separate body, until they joined the United Church of Canada, formed by a union of Congregationalists and Presbyterians. A few of the latter remained outside the union and made up independent churches.

The first Presbyterian church on the island was established by John Hall, an Irishman, in 1861, with a building erected in 1863. He was joined later by Presbyterian ministers from Eastern Canada, and St Andrew's Presbyterian Church was built in Victoria. This church was dominated by the Scottish tradition and has remained so. When the United Church of Canada was formed, St Andrew's did not join, preferring to remain Presbyterian. The Presbyterians founded churches in a number of centres throughout the island.

The Baptists were established on the island by 1877, but initially they do not seem to have been so active. It was not until thirteen years later that there was a Baptist church built in Nanaimo. The number of Baptist churches has increased with the rise of urban centres. The church body does not seem to be as much associated with the rural community on the island as is so often the case in the United States. The Baptists did not join the United Church of Canada and have continued to operate as an independent organisation.

From quite an early period there was a synagogue in Victoria. The Jewish community has never been large on the island, and it has never suffered any form of persecution or discrimination.

The Salvation Army made its appearance on the island in

1887. It was immediately very successful with the Indians, to whom its uniforms and bands gave much delight. The Salvation Army was soon a familiar sight in the streets of Nanaimo and later in other nearby towns. They not only operated churches and Sunday schools, but also homes for the aged and hostels for men. The 'Salvation Lassie' became an ardent worker for the abolition of the saloon and the promotion of temperance. The biggest and toughest loggers, while opposing the army on these matters, otherwise supported them generously.

Today, all of the foregoing denominations still have numerous members and there are other denominations as well to be found on the island. In varying numbers there are Lutherans, Christian Scientists, Latter Day Saints, Pentacostals, Seventh Day Adventists, Unitarians, Jehovah's Witnesses, Ukranian Catholics, Spiritualists, as well as other less well-known bodies. Also, it should perhaps be noted that in Victoria is one of the only two Sikh temples in all of Canada.

Religion continues to thrive, but the function and role of the churches is undergoing much examination. The older generation who are regular in attendance do not necessarily welcome change. The young are not attracted to what they often find tedious and without appeal. Urbanisation has changed the role of some of the smaller rural churches and this transition has often been complicated. Changing attitudes towards the use of leisure must inevitably force the churches to reconsider their traditional emphasis on Sunday services.

HOUSING

Although most of the original Indian villages as such have vanished, a few comments on their form of shelter would perhaps be in order. The aboriginal inhabitants of the island did not live in tepees as is the popular view of the North American Indian generally. Rather, they had wooden structures—plank houses— which were solidly constructed and used for a number of years as part of a regular community.

147

Indian plank house

The planked houses were gabled buildings. The walls and roof were covered with wideboards. There were no nails used anywhere; the boards comprising the walls were lashed to the upright poles. The floors were sometimes planked, but otherwise they were hard earth. The interior walls often had hangings—a form of matting was not unusual—to keep out the cold. The buildings were quite sizable on the whole and were neither unduly primitive nor unsophisticated. Not infrequently, they were sited facing the beach, and this pattern is still seen in contemporary Indian villages.

With white settlement, the traditional log cabin, so much part of North American history and mythology, became a familiar sight. Peeled logs with notched ends were used because lumber was scarce, as it all had to be whip-sawn by hand. The space between the logs was chinked with mud and moss. If there was

148

a fireplace it was made of local uncut stones and puddled clay. Cooking was done over the open fire or in a Dutch oven in front of the fireplace. The roof was made of cedar shakes. Initially, most of the log cabins were only single-room buildings. In due course some were enlarged or extended with the addition of more rooms. Stoves soon made their appearance and these added to the general improvement of the early cabins. Many of the latter acquired chimneys, which were simply extensions of the stove-pipe.

With the advent of the water-powered sawmill, regular lumber became available. While beams and heavy timbers often continued to be hand-sawn, the actual boards were the produce of the new mills. One of the few early structures still remaining on the island is Craigflower Manor—recently completely restored by the provincial government under the direction of Peter Cotton— and this building gives a very good indication of all of the early forms of construction. It must be recognised, however, that Craig- flower Manor is a rather more substantial residence than was common in the mid-1850s when it was built. Most of the early dwellings were relatively small, and it was probably another decade before many larger houses were built.

In spite of the fact that the settlers were of British stock, rela- tively few houses were built of brick. Of course, the super- abundance of lumber undoubtedly accounted for this, but never- theless, considering the natural conservatism inherent in the national origin of the settlers, it is a little surprising that wooden buildings totally dominate the scene. A tour round through the older sections of Victoria, such as James Bay or parts of Nanaimo, give good examples of the wooden houses of the late nineteenth century. Many are quite ornate in external decoration, but inter- nal decor was not very sophisticated. The lack of skilled crafts- men meant that houses so often were built by simple carpenters who were not particularly imaginative. Many of the houses had basements for storage purposes and for the wood or coal furnace. This made the buildings seem rather high in proportion to the general area.

149

Another design that was very popular at the turn of the century was the bungalow. This style was on one level or one and a half levels at most, without a basement. The verandah in many cases was the chief and often dominant decorative feature. The bungalow style allowed for a number of quaint conceits and designs, some of which were not very satisfactory. The bungalow was cheap to construct—one of eight rooms would cost about $1,500 (£600) at that time—and is to be found all over the island, in rural and urban areas alike. Variation on the bungalow style has continued to be a popular form of construction even today.

Residential areas were often 'developed' by building contractors. Architects rarely designed individual houses. Basic designs were accepted and the island is dotted with 'mock-Tudor' and other forms of the arts and crafts tradition.

There are few 'great' houses. Life on the island, largely a life without many servants, simply did not develop in this manner. Housing in the early period was essentially designed to be maintained by the family themselves or, at best, with a single female domestic or houseboy. One of the few examples of the big country house in the Edwardian manner is Hatley Park. This is not original in any architectural sense, but is simply an English country house of the Edwardian period built in 'the colonies'. Hatley Park had the usual reception rooms—library, drawing room, dining room, ballroom and the like—which were common to such houses. In all, there were about forty rooms—twenty-two of them bedrooms. The house, facing the Esquimalt Lagoon, was surrounded by handsome gardens which were maintained by a large staff of mainly Chinese gardeners. Hatley Park cost over $1,000,000 (£450,000) to build. The whole establishment was a monument to the wealth of James Dunsmuir.

Increasingly, houses are built simply for convenience. Central heating is a *sine qua non*—operated by oil furnaces, gas or electricity. Fireplaces have become largely a decorative feature. Most of the dwellings are as uniform as their predecessors. Stucco as well as wood form the exterior and asphalt or other fire protective shingling is common for roofing. The contemporary house for what is euphemistically called 'the young executive' would have four bedrooms, two or three bathrooms, a dining room, a living room and a family room.

It is usual for people to own their own homes. There is little or no subsidised housing as in the British council estate system. To buy a house in most urban communities one would have to pay from $10,000 (£4,000) to $25,000 (£10,000) for a modest family residence. A new house would cost at least $15,000 (£6,000) as an average minimum price almost anywhere on the island. Mortgage rates are high and the government does not give special income tax benefits with respect to mortgage interest. The population is relatively mobile and few families live all their lives in the same house. Two or three moves in a twenty years' span is not at all unusual. It is rare to find an individual living in a house acquired by his parents. There is relatively little attachment to a particular house, but there may well be an attachment to a particular area or community. Naturally enough, water-front property is the most desirable and thus most expensive.

Increasingly, the island has seen the development of the 'high rise' apartment building. This is a new phenomenon. Thus far it has been chiefly seen in Victoria, but examples can be found in Nanaimo as well. This is a distinct cultural change; the majority of the population, however, continue to live in individual detached houses and will do so for a long time to come. There are some experiments with so-called 'town-houses', but these are yet too new and too rare to be important. Certainly, with an ever-increasing section of the population sixty years old or over, various forms of apartment living will become more and more usual. Here the island will be following the pattern of the rest of North America.

MEDICAL SERVICES

The residents of Vancouver Island, like their fellow citizens elsewhere in British Columbia, belong to a general hospital insurance scheme. The premiums are low and the coverage generous. For a single person the charge is $5·00 (£2) per month and for families not appreciably higher. The medical insurance scheme pays for hospital and medical care, but does not pay for drugs. Dental and optical charges must be met by the private individual. However, there are now some private insurance schemes which do include dental costs.

The island is well supplied with hospitals. The two largest, the Jubilee and St Joseph's, have well over 450 beds each. Until recently St Joseph's Hospital was operated by the Sisters of St Ann, but now has been handed over to an independent board. The other hospitals (in increasing magnitude of number of beds) are Esperanza (this hospital is run by the Shantymen's Christian Association and patients are brought in from outlying logging camps and mining claims) (21), Tofino (21), Chemainus (33), Sidney (40), Cumberland (41), Ladysmith (43), Alert Bay (61), Campbell River (70), Port Alberni (111), Duncan (112), Nanaimo (188). The hospital at Alert Bay was long administered by the Columbia Coast Mission, but is now independent. The original hospital building serves as a nurses' residence. In Victoria there are two rehabilitation hospitals, and mental patients can be treated on the island in several places. In addition, there are a number of private hospitals which cater largely for the elderly who require permanent hospitalisation. Patients are charged for these services and the costs are in the area of $500 (£200) per month.

Because of the agreeable way of life on the island, there has never been any shortage of doctors. The latter are among the wealthiest members of most island communities. The nursing staff have been less fortunate. They earn adequate incomes, but they may well be dropping behind the general economic level for professionally trained people. Certainly, no nurse need remain unemployed—probably there is always an insufficient number available to staff the smaller and more remote hospitals—but in recent years relations between the nurses and hospital administrations have been less good. The struggle of the nurses is not only over general conditions, but also over salaries.

152

There is a constant demand for more and better hospitals. Currently, a large building programme is under way. However, on the island as almost everywhere else in North America, even with the new buildings and new equipment, there will never be enough hospitals to accommodate the public. Nevertheless, the present services are of a high level and ought to continue unless there happens to be a severe recession.

It can generally be said that public services—educational and medical, among others—on Vancouver Island are good. To maintain them requires a high expenditure, but local residents thus far seem quite willing to meet increasing costs despite the burden it places on the local revenue.

7   GREATER VICTORIA

To realise Victoria you must take all that the eye admires most
in Bournemouth, Torquay, the Isle of Wight, the Happy Valley
at Hong Kong—the Doon, Sorrento, and Camps Bay; add
reminiscences of the Thousand Islands and arrange the whole
around the Bay of Naples, with some Himalayas for the background.   RUDYARD KIPLING

Victoria is God's waiting room. It is the only cemetery in the
entire world with street lighting.

                              A VISITOR FROM 'GOTHAM'

. . . every aspect is lovely. North, South, East and West—blue
sky, purple hills, snow-capped Olympic mountains bounding her
southern horizon, little bays and beaches heaped with storm-
tossed drift, pine trees everywhere, oak and maple in plenty.
So stands tranquil Victoria in her Island setting—Western as
West can be before earth's gentle rounding pulls West east
again.   EMILY CARR, *Book of Small*

VICTORIA

THE principal city on the island and the capital of the
province of British Columbia is one of the most difficult of
places to describe. Much that is written about Victoria
seems to be the text for a travel brochure, yet, when the city is
actually visited, these descriptions do not appear to be unduly
exaggerated. The general concensus of opinion agrees with the
advertising. True, there are a few carping critics who have been
misled by some of the sham that is inevitable in travel literature.
These disgruntled people have their point too—the emphasis on
the quaintness of the place is unwarranted and the idea that

154

Victoria is 'a bit of olde England' is rubbish. Victoria is herself and has a unique charm. The city is not merely another North American community.

Victoria is not just the city itself; in any discussion of the place it is necessary to include the outlying suburbs of Oak Bay, Saanich and Esquimalt, for they are all part of an integrated whole comprising Greater Victoria. It is true that the suburban communities are corporate entities in themselves. They have their own special characteristics and their own local governments, but they are both supplementary and complementary to Victoria itself. The 1966 census reckoned the population of Greater Victoria to be 157,008, but it is now probably closer to 180,000.

The community designated as Greater Victoria comprises much of the southern tip of Vancouver Island. For the whole area the climate is temperate with a January average of 39°F (4°C) and a midsummer average of 60°F (16°C). Very occasionally extremes do occur, such as in July 1941 when the mercury reached 95·2°F (35°C) or dipped to an extreme low of 3·8°F (−16°C) in late December 1968. The rainfall is moderate—the Olympic range to the west on the American shore acts as a catchment area—rainfall averages 27·35in per year, and snowfall is similarly low. Only once, in February 1916, did it snow to excess, when 46·4in fell in one month. The number of hours of sunshine annually is high; well over 2,000 is normal. The frost-free period of 282 days is the longest in Canada. The chief climatological disadvantage—and this is, in fact, relatively minor—is the prevalence of heavy winds throughout the late autumn and winter months.

The excellent climate, combined with fertile soil and the natural propensities of the inhabitants, means that this is a city of gardens. From the moment that one arrives in Greater Victoria, one is struck by the prevalence of flowers. The 600-odd large flower baskets which hang from the lamp-posts in the city centre during spring and summer are features known throughout North America. The gardens in Beacon Hill Park attract not only the denizens of the city, but visitors from all over the world. Each year the daffodil

155

display has few rivals anywhere. Beacon Hill Park is partly in a natural state, thus combining the pleasurable aspects so desired by gardeners of all tastes. Aside from Beacon Hill Park—which has no commercial concessions of any sort within its boundaries —there are 126 other parks in the area as a whole. They vary from the little native flower garden in Oak Bay to natural forest at Beaver Lake. The gardens at Government House, the residence of the lieutenant-governor, are also open to the public most of the time. These large gardens are relatively informal in nature. Several of the sovereign's representatives have done much to enhance the gardens. General Pearkes, when he was lieutenant-governor, sometimes worked in the gardens himself and occasionally he was mistaken by tourists for a member of the staff.

The population of the city proper is something in the order of 60,000 and is largely British in origin. Since the English are famous for making gardens wherever they settle, Victoria has profited from this enthusiasm. Gardening is a way of life. Indeed, one young man appointed to a professorship at the new university was asked if he gardened. When he replied in the negative his questioner retorted, 'Ah, I take it you are not planning to stay very long.'

The city of Victoria was initially the headquarters of the Hudson's Bay Company. It was formally incorporated in 1862. Neighbouring Esquimalt was settled quite early—initially as a farming centre and later as the Royal Naval base in the Pacific. In the early years all traffic between the Victoria and Esquimalt was by water, but in 1857 a road was built. Oak Bay is a residential community developed from about the turn of the century. Saanich was first entirely agricultural and it is only relatively recently that it, too, has become a popular area for private housing.

The news of the discovery of gold on the mainland in 1858 resulted in a sudden influx of people. On 25 April 1858 some four hundred miners from San Francisco landed in Victoria and the next few months saw many more. Most of these men stayed in the city only briefly before making their way to the mainland;

some remained as permanent settlers, but all of them made their impact on the community. Hotels, saloons, clothing stores, general supplies had to be provided and new business enterprises came into being.

In its earliest years, Victoria was very much an English village with western overtones. It had the ubiquitous dance-hall as well as the rose-covered cottage. The governor was the squire and during the days of Sir James Douglas and his immediate successors social life was old-fashioned and formal. Even today, the whole community is curiously unhurried in comparison with other Canadian cities.

As the provincial capital, it is the centre of government and it has also the Canadian Defence Forces' base. There is relatively little industry; the BC Forest Products have two sawmills and a plywood plant. These sawmills put out 200 million board feet of lumber in 1968. There is also the shipbuilding yard of Burrard Limited of Vancouver. The tourist trade is widely catered for, with numerous shops selling curios, china and antiques. Restaurants, motels and hotels exist in abundance.

No discussion of Victoria could be complete without some notice of the Empress Hotel. This large hostelry, one of the great chain operated by the Canadian Pacific Railway, has 570 rooms and is the largest on the island. It has long been famous for its 'Englishness', and 'tea at the Empress' was a well known feature of Victorian life. In former years, when people imagined the height of gracious living, it was part of the cycle of 'luncheon at Claridges, tea at the Empress, drinks at Shepherds and dinner at Raffles'. One did not have to tell the cognoscenti where these hotels were located. The Empress was long regarded as the haven for the retired colonel and his lady 'from the East'. Recently the hotel has been given a new look, the whole process being called 'Operation Tea-cup'. The principal rooms, as well as the bedrooms, have all been refurbished. Some changes have had to be made inevitably and these are regretted by an older generation of local residents. However, the elegant lobby still retains its Edwardian grandeur and the conservatory remains filled with the famous palms and exotic blooms. The retired colonel and his lady, traditional denizens of the hotel, may be no more, the days of 'the Raj' are ended, but a new generation of guests continues to come to the Empress and enjoy its amenities.

Near the Empress are the Parliament Buildings, a granite edifice erected in the last century. Loyal Victorians regard them with affection and gentle amusement. Locally, they are called 'the Buildings'. Close by, in what is called officially Heritage Court, stands the handsome new Provincial Museum. A multi-storeyed structure in a modern design, it is in stark contrast to the Parliament Buildings and the Empress Hotel. The Provincial Museum was opened in the summer of 1968. There is a also a new Archival Centre which has recently been completed. The Dutch community has given a carillon which is also in Heritage Court.

The principal shopping area of the city is relatively small—probably not much greater than a square mile in area. There are good shops which are well patronised by the local residents. There are the usual general department stores as can be found in any reasonably-sized English town. There are also numerous speciality shops, many featuring imported items from Europe and the Far East. Victoria is also famous for its antique shops, situated relatively close together on Fort Street. Because of the considerable number of visitors to the city, many of the shops cater largely for this trade. Interestingly enough, few local residents go over to Vancouver on the mainland to do their shopping, despite the fact that the distance is not great and since the mainland city is much larger the selection is inevitably more varied. To many of an older generation the idea of shopping in Vancouver is somehow disloyal.

The traffic problem is never very acute, but parking can be difficult. There are now several parking garages to help alleviate the situation. In addition there are now a number of shopping centres which have become popular. Such centres have a number of different businesses such as grocery shops, butchers' shops, florists, dress shops, as well as restaurants and the like. Shopping centres have the great advantage of ease of parking, which in this

158

modern age is considered essential. The chief problem with the development of the shopping centre is that the older urban centre suffers a real decline.

Physically, the city centre itself is a curious *mélange* of architectural styles. There are still a few late nineteenth-century structures to be seen, especially on Wharf Street and Government Street. More evident are buildings that were built between 1910 and 1939. These are generally somewhat uninteresting architecturally, but of good solid construction. Contemporary buildings are similar to those almost everywhere—the cube with large amounts of glass. There are no sky-scrapers in Victoria and a ten-storey office building is noteworthy. Although there are few very distinguished buildings, the overall effect is not displeasing and the skyline is quite attractive.

James Bay is the older residential section. Here can still be found examples of the style of housing of the last century. Recently, a number of 'high-rise' multi-storeyed apartment buildings have been built in this area. Along Dallas Road in particular, and facing the Strait of Juan de Fuca, there is now a veritable wall of buildings.

There are few great mansions anywhere in the city. One such is Government House. This is the third structure on the same site; the first, called Cary Castle, survived until late in the nineteenth century when it was burned to the ground; the building was replaced and then again was destroyed in another conflagration in 1957. It was built up anew and re-opened in 1959. The new official residence of the lieutenant-governor is fire-proof. It is a handsome building, somewhat massive in style, and very fitting as a residence for the Sovereign's representative. It is here that the lieutenant-governor receives official guests, and each summer something like 6,000 people are entertained at the annual garden party. Craigdarroch Castle, with its distinct overtones of 'Balmorality', was another 'great house' in former days. Craigdarroch Castle cannot be dissociated from the story of the Dunsmuir family who were its original owners. Robert Dunsmuir and his wife came to Vancouver Island in 1853. They settled initially at

Fort Rupert and then moved to Nanaimo. Robert Dunsmuir soon began to develop his own coal mining business; his earliest partner was Wadham Neston Diggle, a young officer on HMS *Grappler*. The company prospered and the partners soon became very rich. Diggle sold out his interests to Dunsmuir for $600,000 (£200,000) in 1883. Robert Dunsmuir, now completely in control, began to expand the great enterprise. In this expansion he was joined by his sons, James and Alexander. The latter was to run the San Francisco office, the former was in charge of production in the mining area. Robert Dunsmuir moved to Victoria where he became more and more involved in politics. He started building Craigdarroch and spent a great sum of money upon its construction, but died before it was completed. His widow and his un-married daughters moved into the mansion and Mrs Dunsmuir lived in it until her death. Following her demise, the estate was sold and the house itself put up for a lottery at a price of $1 (40p) per ticket. Uultimately it became Victoria College, later the offices of the Greater Victoria School Board, and is now the headquarters of the Victoria School of Music. Some rooms are also open to the public and it is supported by the Castle Society under the leadership of James K. Nesbitt, a well known local historian and commentator.

Following the death of Robert Dunsmuir, his elder son James became the head of the company. Under his leadership the Dunsmuir fortunes soared. This was the golden age of island coal. James Dunsmuir moved to Victoria and resided in a handsome house called Burleith. He had married an American, Laura Surles, and they had ten children—two sons and eight daughters. The James Dunsmuirs became very prominent social figures in Victoria. Alexander Dunsmuir, who died young, left the mass of his fortune to his brother. This caused a great lawsuit because Mrs Robert Dunsmuir, their mother, felt that she and her daughters had not been properly treated. James Dunsmuir had to go to court to defend himself against the claims of his mother and sisters. After many difficulties he finally won his case, but it was very disagreeable, bringing them all into the blazing light of publicity. Mrs Robert Dunsmuir and her son were never properly reconciled.

James Dunsmuir had represented Wellington in the provincial legislative assembly for a number of years. He became premier in 1900, but was not very successful. He never really understood the intricacies of parliamentary government and he regarded the opposition with much the same hostility that he reserved for strikers and union organisers. Following his retirement from the office of provincial premier, he was appointed lieutenant-governor in 1906 and served for three years. It is now generally acknowledged that he accepted the post largely to please his wife.

After leaving Government House, the Dunsmuirs moved to Hatley Park. Here they lived in a kind of Edwardian grandeur. Dunsmuir was not a happy man in his old age. He occupied himself with a few cronies on his yacht. He died in 1920 and his widow survived him until 1938. The careers of their children can be summarised quite briefly. The elder son, Robin, left Victoria and made his home elsewhere; the younger, nicknamed 'Boy', was drowned on the *Lusitania*. The daughters lived fascinating lives which both delighted and horrified the worthies of Victoria. To *épater les bourgeois* was what they most enjoyed. Hatley Park was later sold by the family to the Canadian government for what was reported at the time as being about $75,000 (£30,000). It is now part of the Canadian Services College.

The arts are moderately well supported in Victoria. There are a number of theatres for films, plays and related activities. Of these, the Langham Court is excellent for the intimate theatre; the Royal Victoria may be considered the principal theatre for large dramatic productions, opera and the symphony; and the McPherson—named after Thomas Shanks McPherson, a millionaire who left his fortune to the city—has recently reopened and provides yet another arena for thespian and similar activities. Regretfully, Victoria is without a professional repertory company, but there is a solid core of professionals and enthusiastic amateurs who keep the theatre alive. The School of Fine Arts at the University of Victoria has a Drama Department which produces a

к

161

number of plays each year. Victoria Fair, which has become an annual event, presents two or three major theatrical productions during the summer.

The city is fortunate in having a symphony orchestra. It has been much helped by the establishment of the School of Music, since the services of competent musicians are more readily available. The orchestra is as good as are similar organisations in similar communities throughout Canada excluding Montreal, Toronto and possibly also Vancouver.

The Art Gallery of Greater Victoria has now been in existence for about three decades. It began its operations in a very small way, and expanded considerably when the Spencer family gave it their former residence and grounds on Moss Street. Since then, exhibition galleries have been built—the Centennial Wing, the Kerr Wing and a third new large wing which has recently been constructed. The gallery has specialised particularly in the arts of the Far East, with a special emphasis on Japan. It is acknowledged that the Oriental collection is second only to that in Toronto and is one of the finest in North America. The gallery also has a sizable collection of pictures painted by Emily Carr, Canada's leading woman artist. She was born in Victoria and spent much of her life there, except for periods of travel elsewhere on the island and for study in the United States and Europe. Her artistic output was large, and her best pictures portray various aspects of Indian life and landscape, views of totem poles and the like. When she grew older she wrote several books—largely autobiographical—which were very charming and droll. She was very fond of animals and her house always abounded in dogs and birds, and on occasion a pet monkey as well. Following her death in 1944, her pictures have steadily increased in value. Her childhood home on Simcoe Street is in the process of restoration, to be opened ultimately as a museum.

A benefaction to the Art Gallery which caused a great flurry in the local and international press was what is called 'The Goya Sketchbook'. These small drawings are the subject of considerable controversy. Certain art experts have stated that the drawings are by the great Spanish artist Goya, while other authorities deny this absolutely. The difficulty apparently is that there are no other extant examples of drawings done by Goya at the period of his visit to Italy for comparison. Artistic attribution is often fraught with difficulty and the 'Goya Sketchbook' is no exception. If, as is hoped, it is finally decided that the drawings are by Goya, the gallery will have received a major acquisition.

The gallery is supported in part by its members—it has the largest per capita membership of any city in all of Canada—and in part by the various local governments in Greater Victoria. It performs a number of services besides providing exhibitions such as lectures and art classes. In addition, the gallery promotes similar activities in other communities elsewhere on the island. Over the years, attendance at gallery functions has steadily increased. The future of the arts on the island is quite bright and the director of the gallery is an enthusiastic champion of contemporary painters, both local and Canadian. The Community Arts Council stimulates the local artistic community.

The city is the base for the Marine Sciences Branch of the Dominion government for hydrographic surveying. There are four such vessels in operation: the *Parizan*, the *William J. Stewart*, the *Victor* and the *Richardson*. In addition, four others are maintained for ice survey. The Department of Transport maintains two lighthouse tenders, the *Camsell* and the *Sir James Douglas*, as well as two pilot boats. The latter serve the Victoria area only. For other deep sea ports on the island, pilotage is provided on request by flying the pilot up to the port in question and chartering a local boat out to the ship. On occasion, a float plane will direct a ship into the harbour. There are also weather ships which make Victoria their headquarters. They are stationed some 900 miles off the shore and report on Pacific weather systems approaching the coast.

The coastguard ship *Camsell* once a year serves quite a different purpose. She makes a voyage with Santa Claus carrying presents to children in remote communities. This annual expedition is eagerly awaited and brings much pleasure to the young.

163

The Junior Chamber of Commerce in Victoria is an enthusiastic supporter of the 'Santa Claus ship' and raises money to buy Christmas gifts.

Two other scientific agencies administered by the authorities in Ottawa are also located in Victoria, namely, the Dominion Meteorological Observatory and the Dominion Astrophysical Observatory. The latter has a 72in telescope—one of the largest in Canada.

There are a number of museums and other similar institutions which attract many visitors. There is a maritime museum in the refurbished Bastion Square—itself a sort of living museum—as well as marine and under-sea gardens which have live whales and other examples of sea life. A very popular tourist attraction is a local waxworks in the tradition of Madame Tussaud's in London. The University of Victoria has a small collection of art objects in a house called Maltwood; the museum specialises in 'the Arts and Crafts Movement', and it also has on display the sculpture of Katharine Maltwood, the wife of the donor of the museum. Katharine Maltwood, herself, was part of 'the Arts and Crafts Movement' and an authority on the Glastonbury Zodiac, about which she wrote several books.

One institution in Victoria which helps to sustain the image of the city as 'a little bit of olde England' is the Union Club, a solid looking edifice close to the Parliament Buildings, the Empress Hotel, the Law Courts and the principal banks. This club, perhaps *the* symbol of 'the Establishment', was founded in the last century and modelled on the gentleman's club in London. While it now admits women inside its portals, there are still rooms which are sacred to the masculine sex. If the conversation is no longer of Poona or 'the Guards', and if the old China-hands and the colonels are in the minority, the ambience is such that if they were reincarnated they would feel quite at home. Traditions die hard in Victoria and the present members, in any case, probably have no wish to alter the comfortable *mise-en-scene*. It gives the illusion that there is some stability in the contemporary world.

Both residents and visitors are able to enjoy a number of sporting activities. There is an ice-rink with artificial ice for year-round skating and for hockey enthusiasts. Rugby, soccer, and Canadian football all find their devotees, both participants and spectators. In summer, there is cricket and baseball, indicators of the mixed cultural heritage of Canadians. Lacrosse, officially Canada's national game, is quite popular. Golf can be played almost every day of the year and there are a number of courses, such as Cedar Hill, Gorge Vale and Uplands, which are close to the city centre. Each year there are a number of tournaments which attract golfers from all over Canada and the United States. For many years the Crystal Gardens was the town's chief swimming bath, but now a large new pool of Olympic length is available.

There are a number of bookshops which sell both new and second-hand items. The public library is much patronised and it has been said that in Greater Victoria more books per capita are read than anywhere else in Canada. Of course, this is partly the consequence of the fact that so many of the residents are retired.

Generally speaking, social life is simple. Although the per capita wealth is considerable, entertaining on a lavish scale, even among the wealthy, is rare. Victoria could not be called swinging at any time and it is unlikely that it would find favour with the jet set. Since it is a society without servants, the general emphasis is on informality and intimacy.

OAK BAY

Although Oak Bay is legally an incorporated town and separate from Victoria, it exists only as an extension to it. There is no indication where the city ends and Oak Bay begins. The locals do say, however, that when they enter Oak Bay they go through 'the Tweed Curtain'. The residents of Oak Bay are noted for their conservatism and it is traditional that on polling day they are distinctly inclined to vote against any change in the status quo. Yet, despite this, the mayor is a woman—the first in the Greater

165

Victoria district—who has long been a member of the council. Moreover, another woman who resided in Oak Bay until her recent death was Nancy Hodges, a member of the provincial legislature and its speaker—the first of her sex to hold the position in the Commonwealth—and later a senator in Ottawa. Oak Bay may not be the home of 'Women's Lib', but the female sex is in the forefront of public life.

Oak Bay is almost totally a residential area. There is what is called 'The Village' and some other areas with shops, but no industry. There are about 18,500 people living in the community. Property values are relatively high—there are very few houses advertised for sale under $20,000 (£8,000), but set against this, local rates and land taxes are low. This is largely because Oak Bay is 'complete', ie, there are no public services such as sewage, electric power and the like which still have to be provided. The roads are already paved and only have to be maintained. There are few empty lots available for new buildings and it is growing less and less rare for one or more houses to be pulled down to enable blocks of flats to be constructed.

Because Oak Bay has consciously maintained an air—even greater than the other sections of Victoria—of 'Englishness', it seems even more incongruous to visitors from other parts of Canada. People still ride bicycles, tweeds are still popular, and pets, especially dogs, are ubiquitous. Indeed, a very famous denizen of the area is an elderly and somewhat morose looking basset hound who daily promenades up and down 'the Avenue' (Oak Bay Avenue) and is greeted by all and sundry as an old friend. Cars slow to a halt to let him amble across the road and he has the right of way on every occasion.

Even within Oak Bay, there are traditionally 'nicer' places to live. It was always thought more elegant somehow to live 'south of the Avenue', but this rather conflicts with the claims of The Uplands to be the area with the most select people. In former times The Uplands was somewhat 'toffee nose', but is so no longer; however, it does have higher taxes proportionally than other parts of Oak Bay. In addition, the street lighting of The

Uplands is somewhat eccentric and certainly not designed for illuminating the roads for pedestrians.

Oak Bay has one of the most beautiful golf links in all of North America—some would even say in the entire world. The Olympic Mountains and the Strait of Juan de Fuca are in the westerly direction, Haro Strait and the San Juan Islands to the south; on clear days, and these are frequent, the mighty Mount Baker dominates the skyline south of the San Juan Islands. Even if one has a bad round of golf, one has superb scenery as consolation.

Oak Bay is the home of at least one of the local cricket clubs. It is a regular sight on Saturday afternoons in the summer to see matches played in Windsor Park. In the winter the same park is the home ground for rugby football, soccer and grass hockey.

The Royal Victoria Yacht Club, curiously enough, is not in Victoria proper, but in Oak Bay. This club sponsors a number of races for various classes of boats in all seasons of the year. The most famous event for sailboats is the annual Swiftsure Race, which attracts entrants from up and down the entire west coast of North America. The course is 136 miles in length; it starts at Brotchie Ledge off Beacon Hill Park, goes out to the Swiftsure Lightship off Cape Flattery and returns.

The race is a great social event. On the evening prior to the race many yachts gather in the Inner Harbour and there is a special ceremony in the grounds of the Parliament Buildings. After the race is over there are many parties to welcome the intrepid sailors home again.

Oak Bay is a maritime paradise, with relatively protected waters. The fishing out in Haro Strait is very popular, particularly when the salmon are running. Such is the quantity of fish in the local waters that almost any small boy can catch a rock cod with little difficulty.

As a community, Oak Bay must be reckoned to have as high an income per capita as any city in Canada. It probably also has one of the highest numbers of people who are sixty years and over in age. Oak Bay is the mecca of the retired population in Canada.

Although many people are somewhat inclined to be scornful about certain aspects of the community, the inhabitants are able to poke fun at themselves. Each year they have a two-day festival which they have named 'The Oak Bay Tea Party' and every visitor is given a hearty welcome. Moreover, one of the highlights is the parade, and the participants often dress in the style of Colonel Blimp and his lady—the archtypal denizens of Oak Bay.

ESQUIMALT

Esquimalt, like Oak Bay, is a separately incorporated community geographically contiguous to Victoria proper. Esquimalt was settled early and acquired a special significance as the Royal Navy base in Western Canada in the nineteenth century. Later the base was the headquarters of the Canadian Naval Western Command. HMCS *Dockyard* and HMCS *Naden* were 'home' to Canadian sailors in the Pacific. Now they are part of the establishment of the Canadian Defence Force. It has been estimated that the local service personnel spend over $1m (£400,000) per month in Greater Victoria.

At one time Esquimalt was a fashionable area, but this did not continue. The general proximity of the service establishments seemed to militate against this. Esquimalt became instead merely a suburb of Victoria. However, in recent years Esquimalt has had a real revival and is once again a very popular residential community. The naval establishment and the army garrison are no longer regarded as mere temporary inhabitants living in rented accommodation. The present service family is very much part of the community as a whole.

During both wars Esquimalt experienced numerous changes. There was considerable expansion of defence facilities, but these have now been cut back. From 1939 to 1945 the shipbuilding firm of Yarrows, now part of the Burrard interests, worked night and day on government contracts, producing frigates and mine-

168

sweepers. At this time there were thousands on the payroll, but with the coming of peace the very large operations were curtailed. However, the shipyard was not closed and still continues to provide a major source of employment in Greater Victoria.

The third suburban area falls under the general name of Saanich; actually there are three separate incorporated communities—namely, Central Saanich, North Saanich and Saanich —with a combined population over 70,000. For many years the whole Saanich area was agricultural; indeed, until 1945 it would have been hard to imagine the area as a residential one. The two earliest farmers, William Thompson and Angus McPhail, settled in 1858. Thompson's son was the first white child born in the area. The first stone house was constructed by William Fraser Tolmie on his farm, Cloverdale. It was here that his youngest son, Simon Fraser Tolmie, later premier of the province, was born.

The Saanich peninsula is sometimes called 'The Garden of the Province'. The soil is extremely fertile. Currently much of the agricultural activity is involved with the export of flowers. Since 1948 over 20 million daffodil blooms have been shipped to the mainland. At Christmas time over 30,000lb of holly are also sent off the island. There are still a number of dairies and some other farms of the traditional type, but these are rapidly diminishing in number. Truck gardening is still an economic activity, but with rising land values as a result of building speculation and ever increasing housing needs, it is hard to gauge how long such work will continue. One is still able to buy from roadside stalls fresh fruits, flowers and vegetables in season, but at the present rate of urban development this may soon only be a pleasant memory.

With the increase in population that followed World War II, new housing developments became essential. Available land in Oak Bay, Esquimalt and Victoria was non-existent on the scale that was required. Consequently, farmers were persuaded to dis-

169

pose of their arable land to contractors and hundreds of new houses were built. The result was that all of the Saanich corporations have been faced with heavy demands for roads, sewage facilities, water and electric power. The old land taxation systems have had to undergo drastic revision to meet the new expenditures. The upshot has been that in the Saanich district the inhabitants have to pay rather higher amounts to the local authorities than do, for example, the residents of Oak Bay.

Within the boundaries of Saanich exist the justly famous Butchart Gardens. These were the work of Robert and Jennie Butchart, who came to Vancouver Island from Eastern Canada in 1904. Butchart operated a cement factory and the gardens are in what was once a lime quarry. There are many local stories as to why Mrs Butchart began the gardens in what would seem to be such an unpromising site. She started to work about 1909 and continued to be actively involved with the gardens for the next half century.

The plan of the area under cultivation is quite simple. There are really four basic gardens: the Italian Garden, the English Rose Garden, the Japanese Garden and the Sunken Garden. While the overall planning was Mrs Butchart's own work, much of the labour was done with the help of her Chinese servants. The gardens are related to each other as well as to the charming house, Benvenuto, that was the Butchart residence for many years.

In the first twenty or so years that the gardens were being developed, many local people as well as their acquaintances came to see what was being done. Everyone was welcomed by the Butcharts as if they were intimate friends. Tea for a long time was provided to all comers totally free of charge. Mrs Butchart, herself, showed people about very willingly and when strangers who did not know who she was offered tips, she declined politely with the words 'Mrs Butchart would not like it'.

In 1939 the Butcharts offered to present their wonderful garden to Victoria, to Saanich or to the Province for a token payment of $1 (40p), but there was no inclination to accept the generous proposal. The lack of funds available to these bodies

170

was given as the reason, but of course the public was more interested in the war than in flowers.

It became increasingly hard to get satisfactory staff and with petrol rationing it became difficult for the Butcharts to live at Benvenuto. They kept up the gardens as well as was possible in the circumstances, but they gave up their old home and returned to Victoria. Robert Butchart died in 1943. His widow survived him until 1960. Their ashes were scattered in the gardens.

After the war was over, the administration of the gardens was assumed largely by the Butcharts' two daughters, Mary Tod and Jenny Chikhmatoff. The latter in particular became much involved, but she knew that the gardens would have to pay their way. Princess Chikhmatoff opened a tea room in 1950; this was very popular, but methods had to be found to make even more money. In 1953 Ian Ross, who was the grandson of Robert Butchart and who had become the real manager, now made major decisions which affected the future of the gardens.

In order to illuminate the gardens at night he had laid 4 miles of underground wiring. He organised summer-theatrical and concert programmes. The Victorian Symphony, for example, gives a number of musical evenings in July and August. Organised tours of the gardens were arranged and the gardens were placed on all the sightseeing routes. Over the years, something over 6 million visitors have come to the Butchart Gardens. Although the sums coming in are sizable, the expenses are not negligible. The summer staff is over 150 and even in autumn and winter something like fifty men are actively employed in maintaining the gardens and preparing for the spring and summer festivities. With reasonable care it is likely that the great garden will survive and continue to be a very real memorial to the enthusiastic activities of Robert and Jenny Butchart.

The town of Sidney—a separately incorporated community, with a population well over 3,000, situated close to the Patricia Bay Airport and not far distant from the Swartz Bay ferry terminal—has developed considerably over the past few years. Sidney has its own shopping area, churches and schools. For in-

171

dividuals who desire a somewhat rural existence, but with some urban amenities, Sidney provides an agreeable solution to their problem. It is entirely feasible to live in Sidney and work in Victoria since at most it is only a half hour's drive between the two communities.

The Saanich peninsula is the only area in the immediate environs of Victoria where much expansion of private housing is possible. It seems likely that the agricultural activities will dwindle. This is sad, since the peninsula is the only satisfactory agricultural land in the southern area of the island. If better planning for domestic housing were established, it still might be possible to keep some of the land in agricultural use. It is really too late to halt completely the drive for more and more subdivision and for increased construction of private homes.

Other outlying communities to the north of Victoria, such as View Royal, Langford, Metchosin and Happy Valley are gradually coming more and more within the orbit of the provincial capital. They, like Sidney, are semi-rural suburbs.

With the prospect of early retirement for more and more Canadians it is clear that Greater Victoria will have more inhabitants. The local Publicity Bureau's slogan 'Follow the birds to Victoria' is becoming a fact at an ever more rapid rate. Inevitably this means a change in the community as a whole. It is a much less intimate society than hitherto; it is much less unique in character as well. The eccentric colonel or the dour commander whose attitudes previously gave colour to the place have given way to the rather more bland typical North American. The efforts by some individuals to retain the image of Greater Victoria as 'a little bit of olde England' are really futile and more especially so when it is so simple for the traveller to visit the original. To maintain a sham or to try and preserve the bogus is to do a disservice to a beautiful and unique city. Progress of sorts is inevitable. The old Victoria is rapidly vanishing, if it has not done so already. A new and very different city is taking its place, but whatever the consequences of the changes, certain qualities will remain. Bruce Hutchison, a local pundit and author, has perhaps summed up these truths most aptly. 'No one who has entered the Inner Harbor of Victoria, so far as the official records show, has ever wanted to leave again . . . This is an island where Ulysses met the sirens. This is the land of the Lotus Eaters, and many of those original inhabitants are still here.'

8 OTHER COMMUNITIES—
Nanaimo and beyond

FOR many years it was said that one only went to Nanaimo
to go to some other place on the island. Yet this was true
only for the visitors, since this has long been a settled community with a viable economic existence.

The bay area has been inhabited for a very long time, as is
witnessed by what is known as the 'Hepburn Stone'. This was
found buried some 22ft below the ground when Hepburn was
digging a well. Archaeologists estimate that the stone was carved
some 15,000 years ago. It depicts a man with a special Far Eastern
head dress.

The Indians were relatively late-comers. The Coast Salish,
who were to make the area their home, called the place 'Sne-ney-
mo'. In Indian language this meant 'house of the big tribe' or
'place of meeting'. The latter form of nomenclature became
appropriate during the later white settlement, when Nanaimo
acquired a reputation as a distribution point for the central section
of the island.

The first Europeans to visit Nanaimo were Eliza and Narvaez,
Spanish explorers, in 1791. They named the area 'Boca de
Wintuhuysen' and it was so called on maps of the period. However, it was not until more than half a century later that white
settlement became a reality.

In 1849 an Indian informed J. W. McKay, a clerk at Fort
Victoria, that coal existed on Protection Island in Nanaimo Bay.
McKay was interested enough to tell the Indian that if he proved

his point he would get his gun repaired at no charge and a bottle of rum as well. It was not until the following spring that the Indian returned and brought down a canoe filled with coal. McKay explored the area and found coal himself. James Douglas was naturally very pleased and, he, too, went to see the coal deposits in 1852. Orders were given to assume ownership of the area in the name of Hudson's Bay Company. Soon after, miners from Fort Rupert were hard at work, and, in September 1852, a load of coal was sent to Fort Victoria.

Douglas planned to establish a community to take advantage of the mineral wealth. The new town was initially called Colville-town, after a Hudson's Bay Company official, but later reverted to Nanaimo, a corrupted version of the original Indian name. The erection of a small fort was one of the first things done following Douglas's decision to establish a permanent mining settlement. The main building, called The Bastion, was octagonal-shaped, made with heavy logs. Two French-Canadian woodsmen, Leon Labine and Jean-Baptiste Fortier, cut the timbers and work proceeded apace. When complete, the fortified area had The Bastion itself and a store, and the whole area was surrounded by a high picket fence. Douglas provided two six-pounders to keep the Indians in order. The guns were used more for show than anything else; they were fired when the governor himself appeared and also on a few occasions when the Indians became obstreperous. Nobody was ever killed with ball fired from these cannon. The Bastion was later used as a local gaol.

The Bastion still exists. It was moved from its original site in 1891 and re-erected not far from one of the places where coal had first been discovered. It is now a museum.

Real settlement may be dated from late November 1854. On 3 June of that year, the *Princess Royal* departed from the East India Docks at Gravesend. She carried over a hundred passengers for Vancouver Island. Among them, travelling first class, were a schoolteacher and his wife; some women coming out to join their husbands were in second class. There was also a large group in third class, including twenty-two Staffordshire miners and their families, ten Norwegians and a widow with five children. The *Princess Royal* took five and a half months to reach her destination. Charles Galt, a mate, kept a journal of the voyage; it is a saga of unremitting gloom, with accounts of storm, sickness and death. When they landed on 27 November, they found conditions that were hardly conducive of good cheer. The cabins which were to be their homes were rudimentary in the extreme, and the weather was inclement, but at least they had no further to journey. These pioneers made the best of it and by the following summer things were much improved.

Within a decade Nanaimo was a busy town. The mines were the source of local prosperity—by 1880 something like 90,000 tons of coal per annum were being shipped, and miners of all nationalities were employed. White men, Chinese and Indians provided the labour force. Churches of various denominations were built, there was a library of sorts by 1863, a local community hall, a school and, of course, the ubiquitous saloons. Nanaimo was a typical western coastal town, with small wooden houses built along the water front and for a short distance behind. The streets were unpaved and unlit, and during the wet winter months pedestrians found them unpleasant for walking. The town was formally incorporated in 1874, a sign that Nanaimo as a community had at last arrived.

Real prosperity did not come until James Dunsmuir and his rivals, the New Vancouver Coal Company, began to apply very modern techniques in their coal mining interests. By 1890 something like 390,000 tons of coal were being shipped out and at the peak the tonnage was close to 1 million. Over 500 men, for example, daily risked their lives going 600ft down shafts and along 10 miles of passages.

Other mining towns in the area near by sprang up to become satellites of Nanaimo. Coal created the settlements at Extension, Wellington, Departure Bay (where James Dunsmuir had his own residence), Cassidy and Ladysmith. Through this last runs the forty-ninth parallel of latitude, the line of demarcation on the mainland between much of Canada and the United States. Ladysmith, founded by James Dunsmuir in 1900, received its name following the raising of the siege of Ladysmith in South Africa during the Boer War. The streets of Ladysmith are named after British generals; there is even a Majuba Hill. Ladysmith was a boom town, where several hundred miners and their families lived. Later, the people of Ladysmith were to become Dunsmuir's implacable enemies when strikes and riots forced the closure of the mines. Coal created the prosperity of the Nanaimo area. It also established a strongly liberal political tradition.

The great days of coal came to an end by 1945. New forms of power replaced 'the black gold' and Nanaimo seemed doomed to become a pale shadow of itself. However, the people were determined not to surrender. A number of unexpected things helped them, of which perhaps the first was the decision of the Canadian Pacific to use Nanaimo as a terminus for its car ferry service to Vancouver. Also the BC Ferry Authority had a ferry run to Horseshoe Bay on the north shore of Vancouver. As a result of these developments, Nanaimo was in closer contact with the mainland and became the principal distribution point for the central part of the island. As more goods were transported by large lorries and vans, the ferry service became extremely important. Although the British Columbia government was to organise ferries between Swartz Bay and the mainland for communications between Victoria and the mainland, the port services of Nanaimo continued to grow.

A second great addition to the community's economic well-being was the construction of the pulp mill at nearby Harmac as part of the Macmillan Bloedel wood products empire. This huge mill employs over 300 men and produces 470,000 tons of sulphate pulp each year.

With its continued economic existence ensured, Nanaimo, with a current population of 15,720, has completely transcended the image of the decaying mining town. Business in the community is booming, domestic housing is being built on a sizable scale, multi-storeyed apartment blocks are not uncommon, and new tourist accommodation is readily available.

The local populace are very properly delighted to have solved the difficulties arising from the loss of their mining endeavours. The old and grim visage of the town has vanished. There is no real regret that the mines have closed. Nanaimo now has a happier future.

Nanaimo each summer commands the headlines, and television cameras focus on the annual bathtub regatta. This nautical or maritime event was instigated by Nanaimo's greatest booster, Frank Ney. Contestants from all over Canada and elsewhere compete in the race formerly sponsored by the Loyal Nanaimo Bathtub Society. Old tubs are equipped with outboard engines for the 36-mile trip across the Strait of Georgia. Many of the competitors wear fancy costumes and the whole spectacle as they approach the strait is fantastic. The best time so far reported for this nautical event was in 1968, when Stan Vallmers completed the run in 2hr 1min.

Another very popular local contest which is marine in nature is the largest mass swimming race in the whole of Canada. This race is across the Nanaimo harbour and competitors are required to swim a half mile to Protection Island. In 1969, 167 individuals took part in this annual event.

North Americans are very concerned about what is called 'culture'. Many of them may be thoroughly antipathetic to most of its manifestations such as ballet, theatre and music, but they often assume an interest at least. It is one of the syndromes of modern society. Nanaimo is no exception to this state of affairs. Outward and visible signs of 'culture' are a small art gallery and an amateur symphony orchestra which gives frequent concerts on Sunday afternoons. Both of these are warmly regarded by the local population who, even if they do not directly participate in either or both, think it right and proper to support them. The consequence is that Nanaimo can be justly proud of what has been accomplished.

It has been suggested that Nanaimo will become an even more active economic centre when and if the BC Ferry Authority establish a ferry service from Gabriola Island to Tsawwassen. This

178

will mean that a bridge or a causeway will have to be built across the harbour. Gabriola Island was first settled by a Glaswegian, John Hoggan, and his family. They arrived in 1854, having moved from Cape Breton in Nova Scotia. John Hoggan was later joined by his brothers, David and William. Today there are some 500 permanent residents. The present ferry service is adequate for them, but if there was an increased flow of traffic to the island the little ferry would not be able to cope. Of course, the rather quiet life of the local inhabitants will be changed should this come about. Private interest must give way to public welfare, but it seems sad that Gabriola Island's future is likely to be that of mere staging post.

Nanaimo has never had the romantic image of Victoria, nor has it been so fortunate in its general history. Its future prospects are brighter than its recent past. As the population of Vancouver Island inevitably increases, especially the central and northern sections, Nanaimo is bound to profit accordingly. Her physical surroundings have been improved by better planning. The Nanaimo harbour will inevitably be used for more pleasurable activities. As C. P. Lyons, in his book *Milestones on Vancouver Island*, observes, 'The blessings of land and sea have been her lot and she continues to grow apace'.

THE NORTH—COMMUNITIES OF THE FUTURE

Once one travels in a northerly direction from Nanaimo, one passes through a series of small communities, many of which are —at least superficially—very similar indeed. It is not particularly profitable or essential to discuss them in detail. Most have populations well under 3,000; only Port Alberni and Campbell River are exceptions with 19,500 and 8,000 respectively. Generally speaking, all of these communities are sited beside one of the other coastal shore lines. Many of these small towns have but one particular attribute that makes them stand out from the surroundings. Port Alberni, for example, is well known for its great pulp mill; Campbell River is the fishing capital of the island, if not of British Columbia; and Tofino, a fishing port on the west coast, is noted for its splendid scenic charms.

The general way of life in all these communities varies very little. The people are relatively unsophisticated, but are generous and hospitable. Strangers are given a friendly welcome, for traditions of frontier and pioneer life still survive. The level of employment is reasonably high and the economic situation healthy. Outdoor activities are popular : fishing and shooting—or hunting, as it is called in Canada—have many devotees. Golf and bowling have many enthusiastic adherents. This is a masculine world and this spirit is very apparent.

There are numerous automobiles, for distances are considerable and public transportation is very limited. Moreover, in all such towns, whether on the island or on the mainland, it is a fact that the car is the symbol of adult life. All youths drive as soon as it is legally permissible.

The new 'instant town' of Gold River is unlike the average north island community. Its establishment was directly related to the needs of the $60,000,000 (£24,000,000) pulp mill of the Tahsis Company on Muchlat Inlet, which was opened in 1967 by Princess Margaretha of Denmark. The new mill was not located in an area where any town already existed or where there was a ready supply of labour. The Tahsis Company might very well have created the traditional 'company town', as was done earlier at Port Alice on Neroutsis Inlet, off Quatsino Sound. The old 'company town' had certain disadvantages, both socially and economically, and it was decided to seek some other solution. Moreover, those concerned with the project came to the conclusion that the new settlement need not be huddled around the mill itself.

The result of this thinking was to establish the new town about ten miles from the mill on an attractive site. Architects joined with community planners to design housing and essential public buildings that were agreeable in themselves. The older tradition, so evident in 'the company town', was to have a dreadful dreary sameness of domestic housing. In Gold River there is a nice varia-

180

tion—certainly all houses are not unique, but there is not a row of houses with an identical appearance.

At present, Gold River has a population of 3,500. There are 218 single-family detached houses, 36 town houses, ie terrace type, and 172 flats. There is also a park for the trailer or, as it is euphemistically referred to, the 'mobile home'. Although the town has been in existence for only a few years, there are pleasant gardens with lawns and shrubbery. The streets are not straight lines, but vary according to the land contour; bureaucratic ideology and uniformity is further restrained in that the streets actually have names rather than just numbers. As a new community in Canada, this shows imagination and concern for personal amenities rather than mere administrative efficiency.

The town has a park which is called Peppercorn Park. The land was provided by the Tahsis Company and the rent was the proverbial peppercorn. Once again, it is clear that the promoters and planners see Gold River as a town to be lived in as well as a source of labour.

There is already an agreeable hotel, with all the facilities which one would expect to find in a much larger urban centre. The local church is an ecumenical venture, being operated jointly by the Anglicans and Roman Catholics. It, too, is attractively designed and in keeping with the contemporary architectural scheme of the town. The school buildings are also very modern —no sign of the proverbial 'little red schoolhouse' of former days on the island—and operates on an open plan. This encourages fresh teaching methods and utilises the facilities to the fullest. No child in Gold River is denied as good an education as is found in older, more established, settlements.

The shopping centre is compact and adequate. Of course, the stores may not be very great in number, but they are a long step from the general store that was traditional in small settlements. People in Gold River are offered the same selection of merchandise as that available in many larger towns. One of the consequences of modern marketing and sales techniques is that the young and old in a relatively remote place like Gold River are not cut off from contemporary taste.

In a way, Gold River is the last outpost prior to entering a closed world. For the next hundred miles and more, the whole area is under licence to various forest products companies. There are no public roads and land communications are curtailed. One can only use the industrial and logging roads at limited times, chiefly during weekends. To take the long drive through the Nimpkish Valley is to experience anew what earlier pioneers must have felt and seen. Emerging at Beaver Cove from this vast un-populated area, one comes almost to another world.

The north end of the island is different in so many ways. The temperatures tend to be lower—on an average, ten degrees—the average rainfall is nearly 70in, and there are nearly a thousand hours less sunshine. The soil is less fertile and the countryside somewhat dull. In addition, the urban communities, when first seen, appear to be charmless and very temporary in character; but closer examination shows this not to be the case.

It is probably correct to say that fishing communities such as Tofino on the west coast have always had all the signs of per-manence which logging towns do not. In the latter, the population seems always to have been transient. Of course, today companies involved with forest products base their activities much more in permanent communities than in the past.

Port McNeill is a good example of this new approach. Port McNeill, named after Captain W. H. McNeill of the *Beaver* and settled early as a result of the discovery of coal in the Susquash deposit, certainly represents this dualism. To some, Port McNeill would be a town planner's nightmare. Part of the shoreline is dotted with houses constructed in the old days by the logging com-panies. Many of them are actually built on large logs which could be floated and towed off to a new site. What might be called the 'new town' on the heights is not unlike Gold River. Of course, there has been somewhat less care in the general arrangements and in the overall planning than in 'the instant towns', and many of the houses are much too close together—although this is an

182

area where land theoretically should be readily available. There are few gardens, part of the old transient tradition, perhaps, where it seemed futile to plant because one would not be present to reap the harvest. Concommittently, it should be pointed out that there are very few animals in evidence anywhere in the entire area. True, there are dogs and cats, and in an urban centre one would not expect to see poultry or farm animals, but neither chickens nor cows seem to exist in any number anywhere. It is another example of the cultural pattern related to former days before the start of permanent settlement. Yet, at Port McNeill, and now also at Port Hardy, one feels that the people are beginning to invest in posterity.

Port McNeill has a school, a hotel—quite new—and a number of shops. It serves as a port, with ferries from Kelsey Bay. There is a good road to Port Hardy and other outlying communities. Oddly enough, although Port Hardy has a population of 2,500 and Port McNeill only 862, the tourist has the definite feeling that the latter may be a more fully integrated community —and this despite the fact that the former is the older town.

Generally speaking, Port Hardy is similar in character to Port McNeill. It has several hotels and a number of shops, but none very large. There are primary, junior secondary and senior secondary schools. All of the major religious denominations that exist elsewhere on the island are found in the community. A number of new houses have been built recently—another sign of the growing enlargement and prosperity of the area. It is true that Porty Hardy has long been a port, but its ambience seemed to reflect the logger rather than the sailor. Life in the town will undoubtedly be very altered if, as is ultimately planned, Port Hardy becomes the island terminus for the ferry run to Prince Rupert. More tourist services will be needed and a wider basis for economic activity will be the consequence. Inevitably, a larger population will be needed as well. The older ways of life will vanish and Port Hardy will be very like Nanaimo.

In all the communities there is a rugged pioneer spirit. The people show less of the refinement that is so evident in Victoria.

There is little 'culture'. However, the commmunity spirit is very vital, hospitality is generous and there is a nice sort of frankness that is lacking in more urban societies. A visit to Port McNeill, Port Hardy or Port Alice is always interesting, but to settle in any of these communities on a permanent basis would not be easy for many people.

The northern communities do not look so much to Victoria, but rather to Vancouver as 'the big city'. Many residents hardly ever seem to visit Victoria, although this can be done by bus and by ferry; instead, they go directly to the mainland. The north end of the island is somewhat forgotten by many who live to the south—the vast majority have never been farther north than Campbell River. The whole area will only become better known when public roads are built to connect the isolated areas. When the projected road between Kelsey Bay and Beaver Cove is completed, the Cinderella-like character of northern Vancouver Island will certainly change.

As an indication of what good communications can do, one need only look at the road from Port Alberni to the west coast towns of Tofino and Ucluelet. It is true that this area has the magnificent Long Beach Park—some 13 miles of sandy beach facing the open Pacific—which is a great attraction, and which has recently become a government park; but even ignoring this, development and social progress in Ucluelet and Tofino in the last three years has been almost greater than during all the previous time which these two towns have existed. The good road —now almost entirely paved—means that the entire area is part of the island as a whole, rather than somewhere that can only be reached by water and is dependent upon tidetables and weather. It is very probable that similar progress—if increased communications and population mean progress—will occur in Port McNeill and Port Hardy when roads are built.

184

9   THE NEIGHBOURING ISLANDS

CONSIDERING the geophysical history and structure of Vancouver Island, it is not surprising that there should be numerous islands lying offshore on both its western and eastern coasts. There are many more islands on the latter than the former, and generally speaking they are smaller in area. The islands on the west coast are found chiefly in the long fjord-like inlets, such as Kyuquot Sound, Nootka Sound, Clayoquot Sound and Barkley Sound. Most of the islands on the west coast are virtually uninhabited, but this is similar to the west coast generally. The few islands that have settlements are those whose population are Indians. Certainly it is true to say that the west coast islands are dependencies of the larger neighbouring island and their economic and social potential are inextricably bound up up with it.

On the eastern side of Vancouver Island the situation is somewhat different. Firstly, there are many more islands and more of them are inhabited. Secondly, it is not as easy to ascertain just which islands can be said to be really dependent parts of Vancouver Island proper. This is more true today, with the vastly improved ferry service to the mainland. Superficially, one might believe that the residents of all of the smaller islands would be considered part of greater Vancouver Island, but past history, economics and population may contradict this fact.

In the past unquestionably, and to a degree at present, the Gulf Islands in the southern part of the Strait of Georgia are sub-areas of Vancouver Island. The Gulf Islands are something in the order of fifteen separate islands, varying in size from Salt-spring Island of 70 square miles in area to mere outcroppings of

185

rock. On the larger islands life is much the same as on Vancouver Island, but on the smaller ones life is still relatively unmechanised. Many of the smaller islands have few permanent inhabitants—some have none at all—and even the larger islands are relatively unpopulated in European terms. In the summer months the number of residents increases somewhat, but the summer colonies on such islands as Galiano, North and South Pender and Salt-spring do not make the islands at all over-crowded. Travelling in a northwesterly direction through the Strait of Georgia, John-stone Strait and out into Queen Charlotte Strait, it is less easy to determine just which islands can be said to be part of the greater Vancouver Island area and which are merely appendages to the mainland. For example, is Texada Island part of the so-called 'Sun-shine Coast' of the mainland or of Vancouver Island? Still more difficult is it to decide the position of the many islands in Johnstone Strait. The provincial department of lands in Victoria, as is shown on the map in its publication, *The Vancouver Island Bulletin Area*, places most of the islands in Johnstone Strait as being outside the Greater Vancouver Island area, but the logic and reasons for this are not given, and it would have probably been just as simple to include them had custom and practice so ordained. However, all the islands off the eastern shore of Vancouver Island, whether properly considered as dependent or not, have certain common attributes.

The islands generally have poorish soil and there is not too much cleared land. Agricultural pursuits are on a limited scale. The raising of sheep is the most profitable activity—the mild winters make early lambing feasible. Water supplies are dependent on wells, and on some of the islands deep drilling for these is necessary. There is also some logging and some fishing, but these are not major industries. Many of the islands have limited roads which are frequently unpaved. In addition, there are few centres that can be considered more than villages. The chief industry is tourism; otherwise, the population tends to exist on external sources of income. On Saltspring Island, for example, over 25 per cent of the population are recipients of a Canadian old age pension of something in the order of $75 (£30) per month per person. While this does not permit extravagance, a married couple owning their own house and a little land can be quite comfortable. For the ambitious younger generation it is probably necessary to move either to the mainland or to Vancouver Island to make a decent living. Often educational facilities are very limited, even on the larger islands, and this impells a move in any case.

To discuss in detail the many islands off the eastern and western coast of Vancouver Island would require a separate volume. Indeed, even to comment on the Gulf Islands in full might require a book of greater length than Francis Thompson's study of Lewis and Harris, a volume published in 1968 in this same series. Suffice it to say that whatever has already been written in this present work on the west coast of Vancouver Island applies to islands there. While this is true to a degree with respect to the islands off the east coast and the eastern shore area of Vancouver Island itself, some further remarks on the islands located here might be useful.

Three islands, two in the Strait of Georgia and one in Queen Charlotte Strait, will serve as illustrations of existence and the way of life on these dependencies of Vancouver Island. The first island to be considered is Saltspring, which is close to Victoria; the second is Kuper, off shore from Ladysmith; the third island is Malcolm, up at the north. Each in its own way demonstrates what could be expected on a visit to many of the other neighbouring islands. Of course, each island community is unique, but there are generalities as well.

SALTSPRING ISLAND

One of the largest islands is Saltspring Island, of some 70 square miles. It was originally called Admiral Island and was so marked on charts until 1906, when Saltspring—which was always the popular local name—was finally recognised officially. The island was settled in the late 1850s. Its earliest settlers were of a very mixed origin; some Negroes who had emigrated from the United States, a few Portugese, and others of English, Canadian or American stock.

Until 1859 all land on Vancouver Island belonged to the Hudson's Bay Company. Settlers wishing to become resident had to buy their holdings; such was not the case in Saltspring Island, for here land could be pre-empted. Thus, the early inhabitants did not need large amounts of capital to establish themselves. There was initially no organised plan of settlement, and people just chose whatever area suited them. By the end of 1859 there were 117 people on the island and the first store opened in December of the same year—a sign of permanent settlement.

Communications with Victoria were not easy, owing to the vagaries of wind and tide. A trip to the capital by canoe took from one and a half to three days, depending on the weather. There were also difficulties with the Indians, who were not so hostile to the white settlers as to the Negroes. Gradually things were brought under control and there were no further attacks on isolated Negro settlers.

With settlement, came outward signs of civilisation. Ebenezer Robson, the brother of John Robson, editor and politician, undertook to hold some Methodist church services in 1861; the next year the Anglicans followed suit and Saltspring Island became part of the parish of the priest in Saanich. A school was established in 1864; in the same year there was a regular weekly service from Victoria. By 1873 the population had increased enough to consider some form of local government—from earliest days they had sent members to the legislative assembly—and Saltspring Island became a municipality. However, such action was premature and was rescinded in 1883. It was not until some time later that local autonomy was restored.

By the turn of the century, the island had a sizable population. From quite an early time the inhabitants acquired a reputation for mild eccentricity. This has not totally disappeared. Of course, in any community with a largish proportion of the residents retired or living on private incomes this is probably inevitable.

188

Life on the island did not really change much until after 1945. With improved communications to Fulford Harbour and Vesuvius Bay from Vancouver Island and with a ferry service to the mainland, Saltspring Island became increasingly popular as a tourist resort and for weekend cottages. Roads were paved and more were constructed, thus making life easier for the local people.

There is a small golf course—nine holes—which is open to the public. Access to the island is via the BC Ferries and also by the Victoria Flying Service. Not far from Ganges there is Mouat Park, with facilities for camping and picnicking. A major feature of the park is Mount Maxwell, from whose summit one can see for miles around and enjoy splendid views of Vancouver Island and other neighbouring Gulf Islands.

There had long been limited accommodation—the Hotel Vesuvius at Vesuvius Bay and Harbour House at Ganges being well known from fairly early days. They were both operated as family businesses and acquired a reputation for comfort and old-fashioned service. Now there are something like fifteen motels, hotels and other places which put up guests. Most are now open throughout the year. To supplement these economic activities, there is a small fishing fleet and some logging.

Increasingly, the agricultural land is being subdivided for holiday houses or for permanent residents. There are now something like 4,000 people who make their home on the island, and life is more and more like that in other North American communities. It is really only another version of what goes on in Oak Bay or West Vancouver. The older inhabitants deplore these changes, but they, too, are not the same. The mildly eccentric English tradition is fast disappearing. The new people are not the retired English civil servant or service type, but just Canadians, and the latter are all very normal.

KUPER ISLAND

Kuper Island is very unlike Saltspring. It is chiefly inhabited by a number of Indian families. True, there is an Indian population on Saltspring Island, but it is not the dominant element of the population. On the other hand, Kuper Island has practically no other settlers. The exception is Folded Hills, a farm owned by Mrs Roy Ginn. Folded Hills extends 100 acres and initially belonged to the Company for the Propagation of the Gospel in New England and the Ports Adjoining in America. This organisation built what is known as 'The Mission', a sort of church and community hall. They also erected a farm house, and it is here that Mrs Ginn resides. Another resident of the farm is a Swiss man named Rene Moeri. He originally bred brown Swiss cattle on the farm, but later these breeding cattle were sold in South America. Visitors to Folded Hills are always made welcome. It gives one the chance to see a beautiful place that is still unspoiled. The Indian community too are hospitable, but very properly resent mere curiosity. They do a little farming, but are chiefly employed as fishermen and loggers. Because of governmental regulations, Kuper Island will not be divided up into minute plots of land for summer cottages. Future generations, crossing over from nearby Thetis Island, will be able to see at least one island in its original state.

MALCOLM ISLAND

The third island, Malcolm Island, is different again. It is partly an Indian reservation and partly populated by the descendants of an Utopian community. In total the population is less than one thousand. At the turn of the century Matii Kurikka (1862–1915), a Finnish political refugee living in Australia, responding to a request from other Finns, came to Malcolm Island to organise a socialist settlement. It was called Sointula—'the place of harmony'. The planners acquired 20,000 acres and the initial settlers arrived on Malcolm Island on 15 December 1901. The conditions which they found were hard ones and the first winter was very severe.

By the summer of 1902 there were 127 people in the community and some sort of life was starting to take form. A few

190

permanent buildings were constructed and the ideals of the community appeared to be becoming realities. Unfortunately, most of the earliest members were urban people—often of an intellectual bent—who knew little or nothing of pioneer life. Moreover, Kurikka had somewhat extravagant ideas and needed to find a way to make the community economically viable. They began to export lumber, but the costs became prohibitive. The final economic crisis followed a disastrous contract to build two wooden bridges—one over the Seymour River and the other over the Capilano River, both in North Vancouver. The bid submitted was much too low and, as a result, the community lost money. Kurikka resigned in 1904. Following his withdrawal a community of sorts remained, but its old socialistic ideals were discontinued.

Today, a small number of people, largely descendants of the original settlers, still reside at Sointula. The children are given schooling at Port McNeill—they are brought across the narrow stretch of water each day. There is a coastal road out along the southern shore for a short distance and most of the present inhabitants live close to it. There is no industry on the island; the men make up part of the fishing fleet based on Port Hardy, or they work in the forest products industry on Vancouver Island. Port Hardy and Port McNeill serve as urban centres for the residents of Malcolm Island and it is in these communities that most of the ordinary shopping is done. Medical services are provided at the hospital at Alert Bay. Life is still relatively simple, although twentieth-century amenities such as electricity, television and the like are not now uncommon. One of the most charming local sights is to be found by looking across Broughton Strait from Port McNeil over to Sointula in early evening, to Malcolm Island in the middle distance and the lights of Sointula. In an area which is relatively without population, it is a very welcome and cheerful prospect.

The numerous other islands are variants of these examples. Their old individuality is being sapped by improved communications. Such is a progress of sorts, but future generations may well marvel as to how untouched life on these islands had remained

191

until the mid-twentieth century. All of the islands will change with improved communications to the mainland of British Columbia and Vancouver Island. The aeroplane has meant that some of the more northerly, such as Malcolm Island, are not now far distant from the metropolitan centre of Vancouver. The isolation of the past is gone. Still, for the time being the islands are not yet integrated into the larger scheme of life; consequently, they retain a very real charm. Of course, the younger generation are often impatient with the lack of urban facilities and economic opportunities; consequently, they leave the smaller islands, as they do in the Hebrides. However, for anyone seeking an agreeable retirement retreat or uncomplicated existence, many of these small islands would be ideal.

10   CONCLUSION

MUCH emphasis has been placed, throughout all of the comment on Vancouver Island, on the importance of communications. Although 1971 was the centennial year of the union of British Columbia with Canada, much of Vancouver Island is still very much as it was when first visited by Captain Cook nearly two centuries ago. If he and his contemporaries were to return to Nootka, they would find it relatively little changed. Yet in the next half century, paved roads and the extensive use of aeroplanes will alter much of this. Vancouver Island will inevitably increase in population, areas now remote will become accessible, and more industries will probably be established. The leisurely way of life will seemingly vanish completely.

The island's own peculiar denizens will undoubtedly disappear, too. It is no longer as different as it once was and, as a result, one of the great charms of the island is gone. Certainly, many of the older residents cried out to be caricatured, but they had distinction and individuality. Now, on Vancouver Island as elsewhere, there is a growing tendency to universality : not always agreeable and often uninteresting.

It is unlikely that heavy industry will ever become a major part of island life. The cost of transport is too high. Great metropolitan centres with industrial suburbs sprawling around on the outskirts are not part of the destiny of Vancouver Island. What will probably develop is a series of urban communities, largely residential with little very light industry. Certainly, those centres associated with aspects of forest products will expand, the more so since the harvesting of timber on the island will continue for

M

a very long time. With careful planning, there is no logical reason why the forest industries should not remain the basic and most important aspect of the general economic life on the island.

Nevertheless, much of Vancouver Island's future is inextricably involved with tourism and all of the related activities. Although a giant in land mass, Canada is remarkably lacking in areas with a salubrious climate as well as handsome scenery. Vancouver Island can provide both. True, part of the island is drenched in rain for much of the year, but even this is better than the snow and ice of the centre of the continent.

With improved communications, Vancouver Island will no longer seem to be so far distant from Saskatoon, Fort Churchill or Trois Riviérès. Equally, it will be in ready contact with London, Tokyo or Ankara. With the apparent diminution of distance as a result of modern means of travel, the lack of great theatre, major art museums, or other similar amenities will no longer be so important. The present isolation which today often seems so very real will be shown to be illusory.

However, Vancouver Island must guard its natural amenities. One thing must certainly occur, and that is proper planning of new housing and general property development, particularly along the waterfront areas. Cheap forms of advertising, 'honky-tonk' restaurants and cafés, souvenir shops with shoddy goods, which are so often part of the tourist scene, will have to be controlled. This is never easy in any society, particularly in one with a capitalistic economy.

While the island can readily absorb a much larger population, it will be necessary to find occupation for newcomers, and an increase in industry on a grand scale is unlikely. Tourism can only employ a limited number of people. It is clear that the island will continue to seek people with capital or with secured incomes to provide yet another base for the economy.

The real understanding of Vancouver Island comes from knowledge of the land. In turn, the land can shape the local life. A tour of the island today will show a rugged land and a rugged people inhabiting it. Aside from Greater Victoria and Nanaimo, which are somewhat different, the residents of the other communities are still pioneers in spirit.

When all of the worst exigencies of contemporary life are considered and the effects on the beautiful island are seen, it is certain that Vancouver Island will continue to be very delightful. Perhaps the best summation of the island's future can be found in the motto of the Province of British Columbia: *'Splendor sine occasu'.*

SELECTED BIBLIOGRAPHY

Vancouver Island, in common with most islands in the world, has quite an extensive literature. To be sure, much of it is included in writings on British Columbia generally. However, on the subject of the island itself there are many popular articles in a variety of journals, numerous official reports and government documents, as well as newspaper items. *The Colonist*, a paper published since the middle of the last century, is a mine of information on topographical as well as social life. Some early works on Vancouver Island are relatively rare, but most can be found in any good research library. The best collection of such writings is in the Provincial Government Archives in Victoria, British Columbia. Here are to be found not only the printed sources, but many collections of private papers as well. Other collections are to be found in the National Archives in Ottawa. The following selected bibliography is of a general nature, but will provide the interested reader with some of the sources used in this present work. Many of these items have their own bibliographical lists and they should prove useful for anyone wishing to do further study.

ABRAHAM, DOROTHY. *Romantic Vancouver Island* (1968)

ABRAHAM, DOROTHY. *Lone Cone* (1952)

AKRIGG, GEORGE P. and HELEN B. *1001 British Columbia Place Names* (1969)

ALSTON, EDWARD G. *A Handbook to British Columbia and Vancouver Island* (1870)

ANDERSON, A. S. *History of Sointula* (1958)

BANFILL, BESSIE. *With the Indians of the Pacific* (1966)

BEGG, ALEXANDER. *History of British Columbia* (1894)

British Columbia, Bureau of Economics and Statistics, *Regional Index of British Columbia* (1966)

British Columbia, Commercial Fisheries Branch, *British Columbia Ocean Harvest* (1968)

SELECTED BIBLIOGRAPHY

British Columbia, Department of Labour, Research Branch, *The Logging Labour Force in British Columbia* (1969)

British Columbia, Department of Lands, Forests and Water Resources, *Vancouver Island* (1967)

British Columbia, Department of Mines and Petroleum Resources, *Annual Report* (1968)

British Columbia, Department of Municipal Affairs, *Municipal Statistics, including Regional Districts for the year ended December 31, 1968* (1969)

British Columbia, Department of Travel Industry, *British Columbia Tourist Directory, 1970* (1970)

British Columbia, Economics and Statistics Branch, *The Pulp and Paper Industry of British Columbia* (1969)

British Columbia, Lands Service, *The Vancouver Island Bulletin Area* (1968)

British Columbia Investments Ltd, *Courtenay, the coming railroad and industrial centre* (1912)

Canada, Dominion Bureau of Statistics, *Eighth Census of Canada, 1941* (1950)

Canada, Dominion Bureau of Statistics, *Census of Canada, 1966* (1967–9)

CARL, G. CLIFFORD *et al. The Freshwater Fishes of British Columbia* (1959)

CARR, EMILY. *The Book of Small* (1942)

CARROLL, H. *History of Nanaimo Pioneers* (1935)

COWAN, IAN M. and GUIGET, CHARLES J. *The Mammals of British Columbia* (1956)

CUPPAGE, EDITH M. *Island Trails* (1945)

CZOLOWSKI, E. *Vancouver Island, a Pictorial Tour* (1966)

DAVIDSON, D. C. 'The War Scare of 1854', *British Columbia Historical Quarterly, V* (1941)

DIXON, L. B. *The Birth of the Lumber Industry in British Columbia* (1956)

DUNCAN, ERIC. *Fifty-Seven Years in the Comox Valley* (1934)

DUFF, WILSON. *The Indian History of British Columbia* (1964)

DUNCAN, FRANCES I. *The Sayward-Kelsey Bay Saga* (1958)

FAWCETT, EDGAR. *Some Reminiscences of Old Victoria* (1912)

FORBES, CHARLES. *Prize Essay: Vancouver Island, its Resources and Capabilities as a Colony* (1862)

FREEMAN, BEATRICE J. *A Gulf Islands Patchwork* (1961)

GOSNELL, R. EDWARD. *A History of British Columbia* (1906)

HAIG-BROWN, RODERICK. *Measure of the Year* (1950)

198

SELECTED BIBLIOGRAPHY

HAIG-BROWN, RODERICK. *A River Never Sleeps* (1946)

HALLIDAY, WILLIAM M. *Potlatch and Totem and the Recollections of an Indian Agent* (1935)

HEALEY, ELIZABETH. *A History of Alert Bay and District* (1958)

HEARN, GEORGE and WILKIE, DAVID. *The Cordwood Limited: A History of the Victoria and Sidney Railway* (1966)

HILL, HAZEL, A. E. *Tales of the Alberni Valley* (1952)

HUGHES, BEN. *History of the Comox Valley* (1962)

JACKMAN, SYDNEY W. *Portraits of the Premiers* (1969)

JOHNSON, PATRICIA M. *A Short History of Nanaimo* (1958)

LAMB, WILLIAM KAYE. 'Early Lumbering on Vancouver Island', Part 1: 1844–1855, Part II: 1855–1866, *British Columbia Historical Quarterly*, II (1938)

LANE, BARBARA S. 'The Cowichan Knitting Industry', *Anthropology in British Columbia* (1951)

LAWRENCE, JOSEPH C. *The South-West Coast of Vancouver Island* (1959)

LYONS, CHESTER P. *Milestones on Vancouver Island* (1958)

MARTIN, ROBERT. *The Hudson's Bay Territories and Vancouver's Island* (1849)

MAYNE, RICHARD C. *Four Years in British Columbia and Vancouver Island* (1862)

MENZIES, ARCHIBALD. *Menzie's Journal of Vancouver's Voyage, April to October 1792* (1923)

MITCHELL, HELEN A. *Diamond in the Rough* (1966)

MOSER, CHARLES. *Reminiscences of the West Coast of Vancouver Island* (1926)

MUNRO, JAMES A. and COWAN IAN M. *Bird Fauna of British Columbia* (1947)

NICHOLSON, GEORGE S. *Vancouver Island's West Coast* (1962)

NARCROSS, ELIZABETH B. *The Warm Land* (1958)

OLSEN, WILLIAM H. *Water over the Wheel* (1963)

ORMSBY, MARGARET A. *British Columbia: a History* (1958)

PEMBERTON, JOSEPH D. *Facts and Figures Relating to Vancouver Island and British Columbia* (1860)

PETHICK, DEREK W. *Sir James Douglas* (1970)

PETHICK, DEREK W. *Victoria, the Fort* (1968)

PYM, HAROLD and IRENE. *Port Hardy and District* (1967)

ROBINSON, LEIGH B. *Esquimalt, 'Place of Shoaling Water'* (1948)

SAYWELL, JOHN F. T. *Koatza: the Chronicles of Cowichan Lake* (1967)

SEWID, JAMES. *Guests Never Leave Hungry* (1969)

199

SELECTED BIBLIOGRAPHY

SHARCOTT, MARGARET. *Troller's Holiday* (1957)

SPROAT, GILBERT M. *Scenes and Studies of Savage Life* (1868)

STAINSBY, DONALD V. 'Vancouver Island's West Coast', *Canadian Geographical Journal*, LXX (1965)

SWANSON, ROBERT E. *The History of a Railway* (1960)

VANCOUVER, GEORGE. *A Voyage of Discovery to the North Pacific Ocean* (1798)

WALTON, AVIS C. *About Victoria and Vancouver Island* (1969)

ACKNOWLEDGMENTS

I wish to record here my appreciation of the assistance given to me by many individuals in preparing this book. I wish to express my thanks to George Newall, Richard Lonsdale and Doris Stastny, who aided me with my research. I am most appreciative of the help given to me by the staff of various departments of the government of British Columbia in Victoria and elsewhere on the island; similar thanks are due to the staff of British Columbia House in London, and to the diocesan offices of the bishoprics of Victoria and Columbia. My thanks to Pauline Martindale, who read the text in an early stage and made most helpful criticisms; to Mrs Norris, who coped with my manuscript and finally was able to type the final copy in excellent form; to Pedro Guedes, for his handsome drawing; to my uncle E. Tatton Anfield, for providing some of the illustrations; and to Philip Whitfield, who made it possible for me to visit some of the more remote parts of the island. I am very grateful for the hospitality shown to me by Professor Brian Pippard and his colleagues at Clare Hall, Cambridge, where much of the text was written. My publishers were very forebearing throughout and for their kindness and understanding I shall always be indebted.

Cambridge 1971   S. W. JACKMAN

INDEX

INDEX

INDEX

INDEX

INDEX

210

211

INDEX